Medicare & You 2017

This is the official U.S. government Medicare handbook.

★ What's important in 2017 (page 3)

★ What Medicare covers (page 31)

CENTERS for MEDICARE & MEDICAID SERVICES

Welcome to "Medicare & You" 2017

Since the health care law was passed more than 6 years ago, we've seen a transformation in this nation's health care. We've covered 20 million more Americans, while providing higher-quality care at reduced costs. And now, the Quality Payment Program, the result of a bipartisan bill passed last year, builds on these improvements. This program helps make sure Medicare doctors are rewarded for providing improved care to you, instead of being paid based on the number of services they order. To continue the progress, we're focused on these goals to help protect Medicare and help you get the most out of your health care:

1. **Providing patient-driven health care.** We want you to have access to health care that meets your needs and is delivered in a way that works for you. Helping you understand your care and options for care is crucial to making heath care decisions that are right for you.

2. **Supporting delivery of the type of care we all want.** This is high value health care, with a focus on smarter spending and keeping people healthier. By continuing to invest in prevention, coordination of care, and quality, we're closer to reaching this goal.

3. **Keeping our commitment to getting you the best possible health care.** We want to make sure that all Americans have equal access to the same level of quality care at affordable costs. We must be transparent in our delivery of care and reduce unnecessary costs and admissions.

We invite you to read this handbook to find out more about Medicare and the ways you can stay healthy. As always, if you have specific questions about Medicare, you can visit Medicare.gov or call 1-800-MEDICARE (1-800-633-4227) to find the answers you need. TTY users should call 1-877-486-2048.

Yours in good health,

/s/

/s/

Sylvia M. Burwell
Secretary

U.S. Department of Health
and Human Services

Andrew Slavitt
Acting Administrator

Centers for Medicare & Medicaid
Services

What's Important in 2017

Stay healthy with preventive services

Medicare pays for many preventive services that can help prevent illness or detect health problems early when they're easier to treat. Ask your health care provider what services you need.

See pages 37–61 for more information. You'll see this apple next to the preventive services listed on those pages.

Sign up for Electronic Medicare Summary Notices (eMSNs)

The eMSN is an electronic version of your "Medicare Summary Notice" (the statement that lists all the services billed and what Medicare paid). If you choose eMSNs, you'll get an email every month with a secure link to your MSN, instead of waiting 3 months for a paper copy in the mail.

See page 65.

Get help in the prescription drug coverage gap

If you reach the coverage gap in your Medicare prescription drug coverage, you'll qualify for savings on brand-name and generic drugs.

See page 89.

Find out what you pay for Medicare (Parts A and B)

The 2017 Medicare premium and deductible amounts weren't available at the time of printing. To get the most up-to-date cost information, visit Medicare.gov or call 1-800-MEDICARE (1-800-633-4227). TTY users should call 1-877-486-2048.

Definitions of blue words are on pages 125–128.

Important Enrollment Information

You don't need to sign up for Medicare each year. However, each year you'll have a chance to review your Medicare **health and prescription drug coverage** and make changes. If you don't have Medicare, see Section 2, which starts on page 21, to learn how to sign up.

Coverage and costs change yearly

Definitions of blue words are on pages 125–128.

Medicare health plans and prescription drug plans can make changes each year—things like cost, coverage, and which providers and pharmacies are in their networks. Plans also can change their provider networks throughout the year. If you're in a Medicare health or prescription drug plan, always review the materials your plan sends you and make sure your plan will still meet your needs for the following year. If you're satisfied that your current plan will meet your needs for next year and it's still being offered, you don't need to do anything.

Open Enrollment Period for Medicare health and prescription drug plans

Mark your calendar with these important dates! This may be the only chance you have each year to make a change to your Medicare health and prescription drug coverage.

October 1, 2016	**Start comparing your coverage with other options.** You may be able to save money. See page 18 for information on comparing plans.
October 15– December 7, 2016	**Change your Medicare health or prescription drug coverage for 2017, if you decide to.**
January 1, 2017	**New coverage begins if you made a change.** New costs and benefit changes also begin if you keep your existing Medicare health or prescription drug coverage and your plan makes changes.

Contents

6 | Contents

Index

> **Note:** The page numbers shown in **bold** provide the most detailed information.

> **Note:** The page numbers shown in **bold** provide the most detailed information.

Note: The page numbers shown in **bold** provide the most detailed information.

> **Note:** The page numbers shown in **bold** provide the most detailed information.

> **Note:** The page numbers shown in **bold** provide the most detailed information.

Notice of Availability of Auxiliary Aids & Services

We're committed to making our programs, benefits, services, facilities, information, and technology accessible in accordance with Sections 504 and 508 of the Rehabilitation Act of 1973. We've taken appropriate steps to make sure that people with disabilities, including people who are deaf, hard of hearing or blind, or who have low vision or other sensory limitations, have an equal opportunity to participate in our services, activities, programs, and other benefits. We provide various auxiliary aids and services to communicate with people with disabilities, including:

- **Relay service** — TTY users should call 1-877-486-2048.
- **Alternate formats** — This handbook is available in alternate formats, including large print, Braille, audio CD, or as an eBook. To request the handbook in an alternate format, visit Medicare.gov/medicare-and-you.

  — To request other Medicare publications in alternate formats, call 1-800-MEDICARE (1-800-633-4227). TTY users should call 1-877-486-2048.

  — For all other CMS publications, you can do any of these:

  1. Call 1-844-ALT-FORM (1-844-258-3676). TTY users should call 1-844-716-3676.

  2. Send a fax to 1-844-530-3676.

  3. Send an email to altformatrequest@cms.hhs.gov.

  4. Send a letter to:
     Centers for Medicare & Medicaid Services
     Offices of Hearings and Inquiries (OHI)
     7500 Security Boulevard, Room S1-13-25
     Baltimore, MD 21244-1850
     Attn: CMS Alternate Format Team

Note: Your request should include your name, phone number, mailing address where we should send the publication, and the title and product number, if available. If you don't know the title or product number, include a brief description of the publication. Also include the format you need, like Braille, large print, audio CD, or a qualified reader.

Nondiscrimination Notice

The Centers for Medicare & Medicaid Services (CMS) doesn't exclude, deny benefits to, or otherwise discriminate against any person on the basis of race, color, national origin, disability, sex, or age. If you think you've been discriminated against or treated unfairly for any of these reasons, you can file a complaint with the Department of Health and Human Services, Office for Civil Rights by:

- Calling 1-800-368-1019. TTY users should call 1-800-537-7697.
- Visiting hhs.gov/ocr/civilrights/complaints.
- Writing:

  Office for Civil Rights
  U.S. Department of Health
  and Human Services
  200 Independence Avenue, SW
  Room 509F, HHH Building
  Washington, D.C. 20201

Want to read this information online?

Sign up at Medicare.gov/gopaperless to get your future "Medicare & You" information electronically (also called the "eHandbook"). We'll send you an email next September when the new eHandbook is available. The online version contains all the same information, but unlike the paper version, it's updated regularly throughout the year. This means you can instantly find the most up-to-date Medicare information you need. You won't get a printed copy of your handbook in the mail if you choose to get it electronically.

Have an eReader (like an iPad, NOOK, Sony Reader, or Kindle)?

Visit Medicare.gov/publications to download a free digital version of this handbook to your eReader. This option is available for all eReader devices. You can get the same important information that's included in the printed version in an easy-to-read format that you can take anywhere you go. You'll still get a printed copy of the handbook in the mail if you choose to download the digital version.

Section 1 —

Learn How Medicare Works

Medicare is health insurance for people 65 or older, people under 65 with certain disabilities, and people of any age with End-Stage Renal Disease (ESRD) (permanent kidney failure requiring dialysis or a kidney transplant).

What are the different parts of Medicare?

Medicare Part A (Hospital Insurance) helps cover:

See pages 31–35.

- Inpatient care in hospitals
- Skilled nursing facility care
- Hospice care
- Home health care

Medicare Part B (Medical Insurance) helps cover:

See pages 36–61.

- Services from doctors and other health care providers
- Outpatient care
- Home health care
- Durable medical equipment
- Many preventive services

Medicare Part C (Medicare Advantage):

See pages 67–80.

- Includes all benefits and services covered under Part A and Part B
- Usually includes Medicare prescription drug coverage (Part D) as part of the plan
- Run by Medicare-approved private insurance companies that follow rules set by Medicare
- May include extra benefits and services for an extra cost

Medicare Part D (Medicare prescription drug coverage):

See pages 85–96.

- Helps cover the cost of prescription drugs
- Run by Medicare-approved private insurance companies that follow rules set by Medicare
- May help lower your prescription drug costs and help protect against higher costs in the future

How can I get my Medicare coverage?

When you first enroll in Medicare, you'll have Original Medicare, unless you make another choice. Here are the different ways you can get your Medicare coverage:

1. You can stay in **Original Medicare**. If you want prescription drug coverage, you'll need to join a Medicare Prescription Drug Plan (Part D). If you don't join a Medicare drug plan when you're first eligible and you don't have other creditable prescription drug coverage, **you may pay a late enrollment penalty if you choose to join later**. See pages 90–92 for more information about the late enrollment penalty.

2. You can choose to join a **Medicare Advantage Plan (like an HMO or PPO)** if one's available in your area. The Medicare Advantage Plan may include Medicare prescription drug coverage. In most cases, you must take the drug coverage that comes with the Medicare health plan if it's offered. In some types of plans that don't offer drug coverage, you may be able to join a Medicare Prescription Drug Plan.

Before making any decisions, learn as much as you can about the types of coverage available to you. The next 2 pages include information to help you with your coverage choices. If you need more detailed information, you can:

1. Visit the Medicare Plan Finder at Medicare.gov/find-a-plan. You can sort plans by plan type. You can compare the coverage, benefits, and estimated costs, and then enroll in a plan that meets your needs.

2. Get personalized counseling about choosing coverage. See page 121 for the phone number of your State Health Insurance Assistance Program (SHIP).

3. Call 1-800-MEDICARE (1-800-633-4227) and say "Agent." TTY users should call 1-877-486-2048.

Definitions of blue words are on pages 125–128.

What are my Medicare coverage choices?

There are 2 main choices for how you get your Medicare coverage. Use these steps to help you decide.

Step 1: Decide how you want to get your coverage.

Original Medicare or Medicare Advantage

Original Medicare

includes Part A (Hospital Insurance) and/or Part B (Medical Insurance)

- Medicare provides this coverage directly.
- You have your choice of doctors, hospitals, and other providers that accept Medicare.
- Generally, you or your supplemental coverage pay deductibles and coinsurance.
- You usually pay a monthly premium for Part B.

See pages 63–66.

Step 2: Decide if you want prescription drug coverage (Part D).

- If you want drug coverage, **you must join a Medicare Prescription Drug Plan**. You usually pay a monthly premium.
- These plans are run by private companies approved by Medicare.

See pages 85–96.

Step 3: Decide if you want supplemental coverage.

- You may want to get coverage that fills gaps in Original Medicare. You can choose to buy a Medicare Supplement Insurance (Medigap) policy from a private company.
- Costs vary by policy and company.
- Employers/unions may offer similar coverage.

See pages 81–84.

Medicare Advantage

(Part C) includes BOTH Part A (Hospital Insurance) and Part B (Medical Insurance)

- Private insurance companies approved by Medicare provide this coverage.
- In most plans, you need to use plan doctors, hospitals, and other providers or you may pay more or all of the costs.
- You may pay a monthly premium (in addition to your Part B premium), deductible, copayments, or coinsurance for covered services.
- Costs, extra coverage, and rules vary by plan.

See pages 67–80.

Step 2: Decide if you want prescription drug coverage (Part D).

- If you want drug coverage, and it's offered by your Medicare Advantage Plan, **in most cases, you must get it through your plan**.
- In some types of plans that don't offer drug coverage, you can join a Medicare Prescription Drug Plan.

See pages 85–96.

Note: If you join a Medicare Advantage Plan, you can't use Medicare Supplement Insurance (Medigap) to pay for out-of-pocket costs you have in the Medicare Advantage Plan. If you already have a Medicare Advantage Plan, you can't be sold a Medigap policy. You can generally only use a Medigap policy if you disenroll from your Medicare Advantage Plan and return to Original Medicare. See page 84.

In addition to the options listed above, you may be able to join other types of Medicare health plans. See pages 79–80. Some people may have other coverage like employer or union, Medicaid, TRICARE, or veterans' benefits. See pages 94–96.

What should I consider when choosing or changing my coverage?

Convenience	Where are the doctors' offices? What are their hours? Do the doctors use electronic health records or prescribe electronically? Which pharmacies can you use? Is the pharmacy you use in the plan's network?
Cost	How much are your premiums, deductibles, and other costs? How much do you pay for services like hospital stays or doctor visits? Is there a yearly limit on what you pay out-of-pocket? Your costs may vary and may be different if you don't follow the coverage rules.
Coverage	How well does the plan cover the services you need?
Doctor and hospital choice	Do your doctors and other health care providers accept the type of coverage you have? Are the doctors you want to see accepting new patients? Do you need to get referrals? Do you have to choose your hospital and health care providers from a network? If so, is your doctor in the network? Can you go outside of the network?
Prescription drugs	Do you need to join a Medicare drug plan? Are your drugs covered under the plan's formulary? Are there any coverage rules that apply to your prescriptions (like prior authorization, step therapy, quantity limits, etc.)? Do you already have creditable prescription drug coverage (for example, through a current or former employer or union)?
Quality of care	Are you satisfied with your medical care? The quality of care and services offered by plans and other health care providers can vary. Medicare has information to help you compare how well plans and providers work to give you the best care possible. See page 118.
Travel	Will you have coverage in another state or outside the U.S.?
Your other coverage	Do you have, or are you eligible for, other types of health or prescription drug coverage (like through a former or current employer or union)? If so, read the materials from your insurer or plan, or call them to find out how the coverage works with, or is affected by, Medicare. If you have coverage through a former or current employer or union or other source, talk to your benefits administrator, insurer, or plan before making changes to your coverage. If you drop your coverage, you may not be able to get it back.

Where can I get my questions answered?

1-800-MEDICARE (1-800-633-4227)

Get general or claims-specific Medicare information, request documents in alternate formats (see page 13), and make changes to your Medicare coverage.

TTY: 1-877-486-2048
Medicare.gov

Social Security

Find out if you're eligible for Part A and/or Part B and how to enroll, get a replacement Medicare or Social Security card, report a change to your address or name, apply for Extra Help with Medicare prescription drug costs, ask questions about Part A and Part B premiums, and report a death.

1-800-772-1213
TTY: 1-800-325-0778
socialsecurity.gov

Benefits Coordination & Recovery Center (BCRC)

Contact the BCRC to report changes in your insurance information or to let Medicare know if you have other insurance.

1-855-798-2627
TTY: 1-855-797-2627

Beneficiary and Family Centered Care Quality Improvement Organization (BFCC-QIO)

Contact a BFCC-QIO to ask questions or report complaints about the quality of care for a Medicare-covered service you got, or if you think Medicare coverage for your service is ending too soon (for example, if your hospital says that you must be discharged and you disagree). Visit Medicare.gov/contacts, or call 1-800-MEDICARE (1-800-633-4227) to get the phone number of your BFCC-QIO.

Definitions of blue words are on pages 125–128.

Department of Defense

Get information about TRICARE for Life (TFL) and the TRICARE Pharmacy Program.

TFL
1-866-773-0404
TTY: 1-866-773-0405
tricare.mil/tfl
tricare4u.com

Tricare Pharmacy Program
1-877-363-1303
TTY: 1-877-540-6261
tricare.mil/pharmacy
express-scripts.com/tricare

Department of Veterans Affairs

Contact if you're a veteran or have served in the U.S. military and you have questions about VA benefits.

1-800-827-1000
TTY: 1-800-829-4833
va.gov

Office of Personnel Management

Get information about the Federal Employee Health Benefits (FEHB) Program for current and retired federal employees.

Retirees: 1-888-767-6738
TTY: 1-800-878-5707
opm.gov/healthcare-insurance

Active federal employees: Contact your Benefits Officer. Visit apps.opm.gov/abo for a list of Benefits Officers.

Railroad Retirement Board (RRB)

If you have benefits from the RRB, call them to change your address or name, check eligibility, enroll in Medicare, replace your Medicare card, or report a death.

Definitions of blue words are on pages 125–128.

1-877-772-5772
TTY: 1-312-751-4701
rrb.gov

Section 2—

Signing Up for Medicare Part A & Part B

Some people get Part A and Part B automatically

If you live in Puerto Rico, you don't automatically get Part B. You must sign up for it. See page 22 for more information.

If you're already getting benefits from Social Security or the Railroad Retirement Board (RRB), you'll automatically get Part A and Part B starting the first day of the month you turn 65. (If your birthday is on the first day of the month, Part A and Part B will start the first day of the prior month.)

If you're under 65 and disabled, you'll automatically get Part A and Part B after you get disability benefits from Social Security or certain disability benefits from the RRB for 24 months.

If you have ALS (Amyotrophic Lateral Sclerosis, also called Lou Gehrig's disease), you'll get Part A and Part B automatically the month your Social Security disability benefits begin.

If you're automatically enrolled, you'll get your red, white, and blue Medicare card in the mail 3 months before your 65th birthday or 25th month of disability benefits. If you do nothing, you'll keep Part B and will pay Part B premiums. You can choose not to keep Part B, but you may have to wait to enroll and pay a penalty for as long as you have Part B. See page 29.

Note: If you don't get your card in the mail, call Social Security at 1-800-772-1213 and let them know. TTY users should call 1-800-325-0778. If you get RRB benefits, call 1-877-772-5772. TTY users should call 1-312-751-4701.

Section 2

Some people have to sign up for Part A and/or Part B

If you're close to 65, but not getting Social Security or Railroad Retirement Board (RRB) benefits, you'll need to sign up for Medicare. Contact Social Security 3 months before you turn 65. You can also apply for Part A and Part B at socialsecurity.gov/retirement. If you worked for a railroad, contact the RRB. **In most cases, if you don't sign up for Part B when you're first eligible, you may have to pay a late enrollment penalty for as long as you have Part B.**

If you have End-Stage Renal Disease (ESRD) and you want Medicare, you'll need to sign up. Contact Social Security to find out when and how to sign up for Part A and Part B. For more information, visit Medicare.gov/publications to view the booklet "Medicare Coverage of Kidney Dialysis & Kidney Transplant Services."

Important! **If you live in Puerto Rico and get benefits from Social Security or the RRB,** you'll automatically get Part A the first day of the month you turn 65 or after you get disability benefits for 24 months. **However, if you want Part B, you'll need to sign up for it by completing an "Application for Enrollment in Part B Form" (CMS-40B). If you don't sign up for Part B when you're first eligible, you may have to pay a late enrollment penalty for as long as you have Part B.** Visit CMS.gov/medicare/cms-forms/cms-forms/cms-forms-items/cms017339.html to get Form CMS-40B in English or Spanish. Contact your local Social Security office or RRB for more information.

Where can I get more information?

Call Social Security at 1-800-772-1213 for more information about your Medicare eligibility and to sign up for Part A and/or Part B. TTY users should call 1-800-325-0778. If you worked for a railroad or get RRB benefits, call the RRB at 1-877-772-5772. TTY users should call 1-312-751-4701.

You can also get personalized health insurance counseling at no cost to you from your State Health Insurance Assistance Program (SHIP). See page 121 for the phone number.

If I'm not automatically enrolled, when can I sign up?

If you're eligible for free Part A, you can sign up for Part A once your Initial Enrollment Period starts. Your Part A coverage will start 6 months back from the date you apply for Medicare (or Social Security/ RRB benefits), but no earlier than the first month you were eligible for Medicare. However, you can only sign up for Part B (or Part A if you have to buy it) during the times listed below. **Remember, in most cases, if you don't sign up for Part A (if you have to buy it) and Part B when you're first eligible, you may have to pay a late enrollment penalty for as long as you have the coverage.**

Initial Enrollment Period

You can first sign up for Part A (if you have to buy it) and/or Part B during the 7-month period that begins 3 months before the month you turn 65, includes the month you turn 65, and ends 3 months after the month you turn 65.

If you sign up for Part A and/or Part B during the first 3 months of your Initial Enrollment Period, in most cases, your coverage starts the first day of your birthday month. However, if your birthday is on the first day of the month, your coverage will start the first day of the prior month.

If you enroll in Part A and/or Part B the month you turn 65 or during the last 3 months of your Initial Enrollment Period, the start date for your Medicare coverage will be delayed.

Special Enrollment Period

If you (or your spouse) are still working, you may have a chance to sign up for Medicare during a Special Enrollment Period. If you didn't sign up for Part B (or Part A if you have to buy it) when you were first eligible because you're covered under a group health plan based on current employment (your own, a spouse's, or if you're disabled, a family member's), you can sign up for Part A and/or Part B:

- Anytime you're still covered by the group health plan
- During the 8-month period that begins the month after the employment ends or the coverage ends, whichever happens first

Definitions of blue words are on pages 125–128.

Usually, you don't pay a late enrollment penalty if you sign up during a Special Enrollment Period. This Special Enrollment Period doesn't apply to people with End-Stage Renal Disease (ESRD).

Note: If you're disabled, the employer offering the group health plan must have 100 or more employees to get a Special Enrollment Period.

Important!

COBRA (Consolidated Omnibus Budget Reconciliation Act) coverage, retiree health plans, and individual health coverage (like through the Health Insurance Marketplace) aren't considered coverage based on current employment. You aren't eligible for a Special Enrollment Period when that coverage ends. To avoid paying a higher premium, make sure you sign up for Medicare when you're first eligible. See page 95 for more information about COBRA coverage.

To learn more about enrollment periods, visit Medicare.gov, or call 1-800-MEDICARE (1-800-633-4227). TTY users should call 1-877-486-2048.

General Enrollment Period

If you didn't sign up for Part A (if you have to buy it) and/or Part B (for which you must pay premiums) during your Initial Enrollment Period, and you don't qualify for a Special Enrollment Period, you can sign up between January 1–March 31 each year. **Your coverage won't start until July 1 of that year, and you may have to pay a higher Part A and/or Part B premium for late enrollment.** See pages 28–29.

Should I get Part B?

This information can help you decide if you should get Part B:

Employer or union coverage—If you or your spouse (or family member if you're disabled) **is still working** and you have health coverage through that employer or union, contact your employer or union benefits administrator to find out how your coverage works with Medicare. This includes federal or state employment, coverage through the Health Insurance Marketplace Small Business Health Options Program (SHOP), and active-duty military service. It might be to your advantage to delay Part B enrollment.

Definitions of blue words are on pages 125–128.

Note: Coverage based on current employment doesn't include:
- COBRA
- Retiree coverage
- VA coverage
- Individual health coverage (like through the Health Insurance Marketplace)

Health Insurance Marketplace—If you have coverage through an individual Marketplace plan (not through an employer), you may want to terminate your Marketplace coverage and enroll in Medicare during your Initial Enrollment Period to avoid the risk of a delay in future Medicare coverage and the possibility of a Medicare late enrollment penalty. Once you're considered eligible for Part A, you won't qualify for help paying your Marketplace plan premiums or other medical costs. If you continue to get help paying your Marketplace plan premium after you have Medicare, you might have to pay back the help you got when you file your taxes. Visit HealthCare.gov to connect to the Marketplace in your state and learn more. You can also find out how to terminate your Marketplace plan before your Medicare enrollment begins.

TRICARE—If you have TRICARE (health care program for active-duty service members and their families), **you generally must enroll in Part A and Part B when you're first eligible to keep your TRICARE coverage.** However, if you're an active-duty service member or an active-duty family member, you don't have to enroll in Part B to keep your TRICARE coverage. For more information, contact TRICARE. See page 20.

Health savings accounts (HSAs)—You can't contribute to your HSA once your Medicare coverage begins. If you contribute to your HSA after your Medicare coverage starts, you may have to pay a tax penalty. If you'd like to continue contributing to your HSA, you shouldn't apply for Medicare, Social Security, or Railroad Retirement Board (RRB) benefits.

Remember, premium-free Part A coverage begins 6 months back from the date you apply for Medicare (or Social Security/RRB benefits), but no earlier than the first month you were eligible for Medicare. To avoid a tax penalty, you should stop contributing to your HSA at least 6 months before you apply for Medicare.

If you have CHAMPVA coverage, you must enroll in Part A and Part B to keep your CHAMPVA coverage.

How does my other insurance work with Medicare?

When you have other insurance and Medicare, there are rules for whether Medicare or your other insurance pays first.

If you have **retiree** insurance (insurance from your or your spouse's former employment)…	Medicare pays first.
If you're 65 or older, have group health plan coverage based on your or your spouse's **current** employment, and the employer has **20 or more employees**…	Your group health plan pays first.
If you're 65 or older, have group health plan coverage based on your or your spouse's **current** employment, and the employer has **fewer than 20 employees**…	Medicare pays first.
If you're under 65 and disabled, have group health plan coverage based on your, a spouse's, or a family member's **current** employment, and the employer has **100 or more employees**…	Your group health plan pays first.
If you're under 65 and disabled, have group health plan coverage based on your or a family member's **current** employment, and the employer has **fewer than 100 employees**…	Medicare pays first.
If you have Medicare because of End-Stage Renal Disease (ESRD)…	Your group health plan will pay first for the first 30 months after you become eligible to enroll in Medicare. Medicare will pay first after this 30-month period.

Definitions of blue words are on pages 125–128.

Note: In some cases, your employer may join with other employers or unions to form or sponsor a multiple-employer plan. If this happens, the size of the largest employer/union determines whether Medicare pays first or second.

Here are some important facts to remember:

- The insurance that pays first (primary payer) pays up to the limits of its coverage.
- The insurance that pays second (secondary payer) only pays if there are costs the primary insurer didn't cover.
- The secondary payer (which may be Medicare) might not pay all of the uncovered costs.
- If your employer insurance is the secondary payer, you might need to enroll in Part B before your insurance will pay.

For more information, visit Medicare.gov/publications to view the booklet "Medicare & Other Health Benefits: Your Guide to Who Pays First."

Important! If you have other insurance, be sure to tell your health care provider, hospital, and pharmacy. You'll also need to let Medicare know by calling Medicare's Benefits Coordination & Recovery Center (BCRC) at 1-855-798-2627. TTY users should call 1-855-797-2627.

Important! If you have Medicare Part A (including coverage in a Medicare Advantage Plan), you meet the requirement for having health coverage under the Affordable Care Act. This means you won't have to pay a penalty when you file your federal tax return.

If you have Part A, you may get a Health Coverage form (IRS Form 1095-B) from Medicare by early 2017. This form verifies that you had health coverage, and you'll have to report this on your federal income tax return. Keep the form for your records.

How much does Part A coverage cost?

You usually don't pay a monthly premium for Part A coverage if you or your spouse paid Medicare taxes while working. This is sometimes called premium-free Part A. If you aren't eligible for premium-free Part A, you may be able to buy Part A.

In most cases, if you choose to **buy** Part A, you must also have Part B and pay monthly premiums for both.

The 2017 Part A premium amounts weren't available at the time of printing. To get the most up-to-date cost information, visit Medicare.gov or call 1-800-MEDICARE. TTY users should call 1-877-486-2048.

What's the Part A late enrollment penalty?

If you aren't eligible for premium-free Part A, and you don't buy it when you're first eligible, your monthly premium may go up 10%. You'll have to pay the higher premium for twice the number of years you could've had Part A, but didn't sign up.

> **Example:** If you were eligible for Part A for 2 years but didn't sign up, you'll have to pay a 10% higher premium for 4 years.

How much does Part B coverage cost?

In 2016, the standard Part B premium amount was $121.80 (or higher depending on your income). However, most people who get Social Security benefits continued to pay the same Part B premium amount as they paid in 2015 unless:

- You enrolled in Part B for the first time in 2016.
- You don't get Social Security benefits.
- You're directly billed for your Part B premiums.
- You have Medicare and Medicaid, and Medicaid pays your premiums. (Your state will pay the standard premium amount of $121.80.)
- Your modified adjusted gross income as reported on your IRS tax return from 2 years ago is above a certain amount ($85,000 if you file individually or $170,000 if you're married and file jointly).

The 2017 premium amount wasn't available at the time of printing. To get the most up-to-date cost information, visit Medicare.gov or call 1-800-MEDICARE. TTY users should call 1-877-486-2048.

What's the Part B late enrollment penalty?

If you don't sign up for Part B when you're first eligible, you may have to pay a late enrollment penalty for as long as you have Part B. Your monthly premium for Part B may go up 10% for each full 12-month period that you could've had Part B, but didn't sign up for it. If you're allowed to sign up for Part B during a Special Enrollment Period, you usually don't pay a late enrollment penalty. See pages 23–24.

Example: Mr. Smith's Initial Enrollment Period ended September 30, 2013. He waited to sign up for Part B until March 2016 during the General Enrollment Period. His Part B premium penalty is 20%, and he'll have to pay this penalty for as long as he has Part B. (Even though Mr. Smith waited a total of 30 months to sign up, this included only 2 full 12-month periods.)

How can I pay my Part B premium?

If you get Social Security, Railroad Retirement Board (RRB), or Office of Personnel Management (OPM) benefits, your Part B premium will be automatically deducted from your benefit payment. If you don't get these benefit payments, you'll get a bill. If you choose to buy Part A, you'll always get a bill for your premium. There are 4 ways to pay these bills:

1. Mail your premium payments to:

   Medicare Premium Collection Center
   P.O. Box 790355
   St. Louis, Missouri 63179-0355

   If you get a bill from the RRB, mail your premium payments to:
   RRB
   Medicare Premium Payments
   P.O. Box 979024
   St. Louis, Missouri 63197-9000

2. Pay by credit/debit card. To do this, complete the bottom portion of the payment coupon on your Medicare bill and mail it to the address above.

Definitions of blue words are on pages 125–128.

3. Sign up for Medicare Easy Pay. This is a free service that automatically deducts your premium payments from your savings or checking account each month. Visit Medicare.gov or call 1-800-MEDICARE (1-800-633-4227) to learn more and to find out how to sign up. TTY users should call 1-877-486-2048.

4. Make an online bill payment. This is a more secure and faster way to make your payment without sending your personal information in the mail. Ask your bank if it allows customers to pay bills online. Not all banks offer this service and some may charge a fee. You'll need to give the bank this information:

   ▪ Account number: Your Medicare claim number without dashes (you'll find this number on your red, white, and blue Medicare card).
   ▪ Biller name: CMS Medicare Insurance
   ▪ Remittance address:
     Medicare Premium Collection Center
     P.O. Box 790355
     St. Louis, Missouri 63179-0355

If you have questions about your premiums or need to change your address on your bill, call Social Security at 1-800-772-1213. TTY users should call 1-800-325-0778. If your bills are from the RRB, call 1-877-772-5772. TTY users should call 1-312-751-4701.

Section 3 —

Find Out if Medicare Covers Your Test, Service, or Item

What services does Medicare cover?

Medicare covers certain medical services and supplies in hospitals, doctors' offices, and other health care settings. Services are either covered under Part A or Part B.

If you have both Part A and Part B, you can get all of the Medicare-covered services listed in this section, whether you have Original Medicare or a Medicare Advantage Plan (like an HMO or PPO).

Important! To get Medicare-covered Part A and/or Part B services, you must be a U.S. citizen or be lawfully present in the U.S.

What does Part A cover?

Part A (Hospital Insurance) helps cover:

- Inpatient care in a hospital
- Inpatient care in a skilled nursing facility (not custodial or long-term care)
- Hospice care
- Home health care
- Inpatient care in a religious nonmedical health care institution

You can find out if you have Part A by looking at your red, white, and blue Medicare card. If you have Original Medicare, you'll use this card to get your Medicare-covered services. If you join a Medicare Advantage Plan, in most cases, you must use the card from the plan to get your Medicare-covered services.

What do I pay for Part A-covered services?

Copayments, coinsurance, or deductibles may apply for each service listed on the following pages. Visit Medicare.gov, or call 1-800-MEDICARE (1-800-633-4227) to get specific cost information. TTY users should call 1-877-486-2048.

If you're in a Medicare Advantage Plan or have other insurance (like a Medicare Supplement Insurance (Medigap) policy, or employer or union coverage), your costs may be different. Contact the plans you're interested in to find out about the costs, or visit the Medicare Plan Finder at Medicare.gov/find-a-plan.

Part A-covered services

Blood

If the hospital gets blood from a blood bank at no charge, you won't have to pay for it or replace it. If the hospital has to buy blood for you, you must either pay the hospital costs for the first 3 units of blood you get in a calendar year or have the blood donated by you or someone else.

Home health services

You can use your home health benefits under Part A and/or Part B. See page 50 for more information about home health benefits.

Hospice care

To qualify for hospice care, a hospice doctor and your doctor (if you have one) must certify that you're terminally ill, meaning you have a life expectancy of 6 months or less. If you're already getting hospice care, a hospice doctor or nurse practitioner will need to see you about 6 months after your hospice care started to certify that you're still terminally ill. Coverage includes:

- All items and services needed for pain relief and symptom management
- Medical, nursing, and social services
- Drugs
- Certain durable medical equipment
- Aide and homemaker services

- Other covered services, as well as services Medicare usually doesn't cover, like spiritual and grief counseling

A Medicare-approved hospice usually gives hospice care in your home or other facility where you live, like a nursing home.

Hospice care doesn't pay for your stay in a facility (room and board) unless the hospice medical team determines that you need short-term inpatient stays for pain and symptom management that can't be addressed at home. These stays must be in a Medicare-approved facility, like a hospice facility, hospital, or skilled nursing facility that contracts with the hospice. Medicare also covers inpatient respite care, which is care you get in a Medicare-approved facility so that your usual caregiver (family member or friend) can rest. You can stay up to 5 days each time you get respite care. Medicare will pay for covered services for health problems that aren't related to your terminal illness or related conditions. You can continue to get hospice care as long as the hospice medical director or hospice doctor recertifies that you're terminally ill.

- You pay nothing for hospice care.
- You pay a copayment of up to $5 per prescription for outpatient prescription drugs for pain and symptom management. In the rare case your drug isn't covered by the hospice benefit, your hospice provider should contact your Medicare drug plan to see if it's covered under Part D.
- You pay 5% of the Medicare-approved amount for inpatient respite care.

Hospital care (inpatient care)

Medicare covers semi-private rooms, meals, general nursing, and drugs as part of your inpatient treatment, and other hospital services and supplies. This includes care you get in acute care hospitals, critical access hospitals, inpatient rehabilitation facilities, long-term care hospitals, inpatient care as part of a qualifying clinical research study, and mental health care. This doesn't include private-duty nursing, a television or phone in your room (if there's a separate charge for these items), or personal care items, like razors or slipper socks. It also doesn't include a private room, unless medically necessary. If you have Part B, it generally covers 80% of the Medicare-approved amount for doctor's services you get while you're in a hospital.

Definitions of blue words are on pages 125–128.

- You pay a deductible and no coinsurance for days 1–60 of each benefit period.
- You pay coinsurance for days 61–90 of each benefit period.
- You pay coinsurance per "lifetime reserve day" after day 90 of each benefit period (up to 60 days over your lifetime).
- You pay all costs for each day after you use all the lifetime reserve days.
- Inpatient psychiatric care in a freestanding psychiatric hospital is limited to 190 days in a lifetime.

Note: In some cases, the hospital or a Medicare contractor may determine you should've gotten services in an outpatient setting. The hospital may submit a Part B claim for your services, and the amount you owe may change. You'll pay your part for Part B services, but you may be able to get a refund for any money you paid for Part A services.

Am I an inpatient or outpatient?

Staying overnight in a hospital doesn't always mean you're an inpatient. You only become an inpatient when a hospital formally admits you as an inpatient, after a doctor orders it. You're still an outpatient if you haven't been formally admitted as an inpatient, even if you're getting emergency department services, observation services, outpatient surgery, lab tests, or X-rays. **You or a family member should always ask if you're an inpatient or an outpatient each day during your stay, since it affects what you pay and can affect whether you'll qualify for Part A coverage in a skilled nursing facility.**

Religious non-medical health care institution (inpatient care)

In these facilities, religious beliefs prohibit conventional and unconventional medical care. If you qualify for hospital or skilled nursing facility care, Medicare will only cover the inpatient, non-religious, non-medical items and services. Examples are room and board, or any items and services that don't require a doctor's order or prescription, like unmedicated wound dressings or use of a simple walker.

Skilled nursing facility care

Medicare covers semi-private rooms, meals, skilled nursing and rehabilitative services, and other medically necessary services and supplies after a 3-day minimum, medically necessary, inpatient hospital stay for a related illness or injury. An inpatient hospital stay begins the day the hospital formally admits you as an inpatient based on a doctor's order and doesn't include the day you're discharged. You may get coverage of skilled nursing care or skilled therapy care if it's necessary to:

- Help improve your condition

  or

- Maintain your current condition or prevent or delay it from getting worse

To qualify for care in a skilled nursing facility, your doctor must certify that you need daily skilled care like intravenous injections or physical therapy.

You pay:

- Nothing for the first 20 days of each benefit period
- A coinsurance per day for days 21–100 of each benefit period
- All costs for each day after day 100 in a benefit period

Visit Medicare.gov, or call 1-800-MEDICARE (1-800-633-4227) to find out what you pay for inpatient hospital stays and skilled nursing facility care in 2017. TTY users should call 1-877-486-2048.

Note: Medicare doesn't cover long-term care or custodial care.

Definitions of blue words are on pages 125–128.

What does Part B cover?

Medicare Part B (Medical Insurance) helps cover medically necessary doctors' services, outpatient care, home health services, durable medical equipment, and other medical services. Part B also covers many preventive services. You can find out if you have Part B by looking at your red, white, and blue Medicare card. See pages 37–61 for a list of common Part B-covered services and general descriptions. Medicare may cover some services and tests more often than the timeframes listed if needed to diagnose or treat a condition. To find out if Medicare covers a service not on this list, visit Medicare.gov/coverage, or call 1-800-MEDICARE (1-800-633-4227). TTY users should call 1-877-486-2048. For more details about Medicare covered services, visit Medicare.gov/publications to view the booklet "Your Medicare Benefits." Call 1-800-MEDICARE to find out if a copy can be mailed to you.

What do I pay for Part B-covered services?

The alphabetical list on the following pages gives general information about what you pay if you have Original Medicare and see doctors or other health care providers who accept assignment. See page 66. You'll pay more if you see doctors or providers who don't accept assignment. **If you're in a Medicare Advantage Plan (like an HMO or PPO) or have other insurance, your costs may be different. Contact your plan or benefits administrator directly to find out about the costs.**

Under Original Medicare, if the Part B deductible ($166 in 2016) applies, you must pay all costs (up to the Medicare-approved amount) until you meet the yearly Part B deductible before Medicare begins to pay its share. Then, after your deductible is met, you typically pay 20% of the Medicare-approved amount of the service, if the doctor or other health care provider accepts assignment. There's no yearly limit for what you pay out-of-pocket. Visit Medicare.gov or call 1-800-MEDICARE to get specific cost information.

You pay nothing for most covered preventive services if you get the services from a doctor or other qualified health care provider who accepts assignment. However, for some preventive services, you may have to pay a deductible, coinsurance, or both. These costs may also apply if you get a preventive service in the same visit as a non-preventive service.

Definitions of blue words are on pages 125–128.

Part B-covered services

 You'll see this apple next to the preventive services on pages 37–61.

Abdominal aortic aneurysm screening

Medicare covers a one-time screening abdominal aortic aneurysm ultrasound for people at risk. You must get a referral from your doctor or other practitioner. You pay nothing for the screening if the doctor or other qualified health care provider accepts assignment.

Note: If you have a family history of abdominal aortic aneurysms, or you're a man 65–75 and you've smoked at least 100 cigarettes in your lifetime, you're considered at risk.

Advance Care Planning

Medicare covers voluntary Advance Care Planning as part of the Yearly "Wellness" visit. This is planning for care you would want to get if you become unable to speak for yourself. You can talk about an advance directive with your health care professional, and he or she can help you fill out the forms, if you want to. An advance directive is a legal document that records your wishes about medical treatment at a future time, if you're not able to make decisions about your care. You pay nothing if the doctor or other qualified health care provider accepts assignment.

Note: Medicare may also cover this service as part of your medical treatment. When Advance Care Planning isn't part of your Annual "Wellness" visit, the Part B deductible and coinsurance apply.

Alcohol misuse screening and counseling

Medicare covers one alcohol misuse screening per year for adults with Medicare (including pregnant women) who use alcohol, but don't meet the medical criteria for alcohol dependency. If your primary care doctor or other primary care practitioner determines you're misusing alcohol, you can get up to 4 brief face-to-face counseling sessions per year (if you're competent and alert during counseling). A qualified primary care doctor or other primary care practitioner must provide the counseling in a primary care setting (like a doctor's office). You pay nothing if the qualified primary care doctor or other primary care practitioner accepts assignment.

Ambulance services

Medicare covers ground ambulance transportation when you need to be transported to a hospital, critical access hospital, or skilled nursing facility for medically necessary services, and transportation in any other vehicle could endanger your health. Medicare may pay for emergency ambulance transportation in an airplane or helicopter to a hospital if you need immediate and rapid ambulance transportation that ground transportation can't provide.

In some cases, Medicare may pay for limited, medically necessary, non-emergency ambulance transportation if you have a written order from your doctor stating that ambulance transportation is medically necessary. An example may be a medically necessary ambulance transport to a renal dialysis facility for an End-Stage Renal Disease (ESRD) patient.

Medicare will only cover ambulance services to the nearest appropriate medical facility that's able to give you the care you need.

You pay 20% of the Medicare-approved amount, and the Part B deductible applies.

Ambulatory surgical centers

Medicare covers the facility service fees related to approved surgical procedures provided in an ambulatory surgical center (facility where surgical procedures are performed, and the patient is expected to be released within 24 hours). Except for certain preventive services (for which you pay nothing if the doctor or other health care provider accepts assignment), you pay 20% of the Medicare-approved amount to both the ambulatory surgical center and the doctor who treats you, and the Part B deductible applies. You pay all of the facility service fees for procedures Medicare doesn't cover in ambulatory surgical centers.

Blood

If the provider gets blood from a blood bank at no charge, you won't have to pay for it or replace it. However, you'll pay a copayment for the blood processing and handling services for each unit of blood you get, and the Part B deductible applies. If the provider has to buy blood for you, you must either pay the provider costs for the first 3 units of blood you get in a calendar year or have the blood donated by you or someone else.

Definitions of blue words are on pages 125–128.

Bone mass measurement (bone density)

This test helps to see if you're at risk for broken bones. It's covered once every 24 months (more often if medically necessary) for people who have certain medical conditions or meet certain criteria. You pay nothing for this test if the doctor or other qualified health care provider accepts assignment.

Breast cancer screening (mammograms)

Medicare covers screening mammograms to check for breast cancer once every 12 months for all women with Medicare who are 40 and older. Medicare covers one baseline mammogram for women between 35–39. You pay nothing for the test if the doctor or other qualified health care provider accepts assignment.

Note: Part B also covers diagnostic mammograms more frequently than once a year when medically necessary. You pay 20% of the Medicare-approved amount for diagnostic mammograms, and the Part B deductible applies.

Cardiac rehabilitation

Medicare covers comprehensive programs that include exercise, education, and counseling for patients who meet at least one of these conditions:
- A heart attack in the last 12 months
- Coronary artery bypass surgery
- Current stable angina pectoris (chest pain)
- A heart valve repair or replacement
- A coronary angioplasty (a medical procedure used to open a blocked artery) or coronary stenting (a procedure used to keep an artery open)
- A heart or heart-lung transplant

Medicare also covers intensive cardiac rehabilitation programs that are typically more rigorous or more intense than regular cardiac rehabilitation programs. Services are covered in a doctor's office or hospital outpatient setting. You pay 20% of the Medicare-approved amount if you get the services in a doctor's office. In a hospital outpatient setting, you also pay the hospital a copayment. The Part B deductible applies.

Cardiovascular disease (behavioral therapy)

Medicare will cover one visit per year with a primary care doctor in a primary care setting (like a doctor's office) to help lower your risk for cardiovascular disease. During this visit, the doctor may discuss aspirin use (if appropriate), check your blood pressure, and give you tips to make sure you eat well. You pay nothing if the doctor or other qualified health care provider accepts assignment.

Cardiovascular disease screenings

These screenings include blood tests that help detect conditions that may lead to a heart attack or stroke. Medicare covers these screening tests once every 5 years to test your cholesterol, lipid, lipoprotein, and triglyceride levels. You pay nothing for the tests if the doctor or other qualified health care provider accepts assignment.

Cervical and vaginal cancer screenings

Part B covers Pap tests and pelvic exams to check for cervical and vaginal cancers. As part of the pelvic exam, Medicare also covers a clinical breast exam to check for breast cancer. Medicare covers these screening tests once every 24 months. Medicare covers these screening tests once every 12 months if you're at high risk for cervical or vaginal cancer, or if you're of child-bearing age and had an abnormal Pap test in the past 36 months.

Part B also covers Human Papillomavirus (HPV) tests (when received with a Pap test) once every 5 years if you're age 30–65 without HPV symptoms.

You pay nothing for the lab Pap test or for the lab HPV with Pap test if your doctor or other qualified health care provider accepts assignment. You also pay nothing for the Pap test specimen collection and pelvic and breast exams if the doctor or other qualified health care provider accepts assignment.

Chemotherapy

Medicare covers chemotherapy in a doctor's office, freestanding clinic, or hospital outpatient setting for people with cancer. You pay a copayment for chemotherapy in a hospital outpatient setting.

For chemotherapy given in a doctor's office or freestanding clinic, you pay 20% of the Medicare-approved amount, and the Part B deductible applies.

For chemotherapy in a hospital inpatient setting covered under Part A, see Hospital care (inpatient care) on page 33–34.

Chiropractic services (limited coverage)

Medicare covers manipulation of the spine if medically necessary to correct a subluxation (when one or more of the bones of your spine move out of position) when provided by a chiropractor or other qualified provider. You pay 20% of the Medicare-approved amount, and the Part B deductible applies.

Note: You pay all costs for any other services or tests ordered by a chiropractor (including X-rays and massage therapy).

Chronic Care Management Services

If you have 2 or more chronic conditions that are expected to last at least a year, Medicare may pay for a health care provider's help to manage those conditions. This includes a comprehensive care plan that lists your health problems and goals, other health care providers, medications, community services you have and need, and other information about your health. It also explains the care you need and how your care will be coordinated. A chronic condition could be arthritis, asthma, diabetes, hypertension, heart disease, osteoporosis, and other conditions. Your health care provider will ask you to sign an agreement to provide this service. If you agree, he or she will prepare the care plan, help you with medication management, provide 24/7 access for urgent care needs, give you support when you go from one health care setting to another, review your medicines and how you take them, and help you with other chronic care needs. There's a monthly fee, and the Part B deductible and coinsurance apply.

Definitions of blue words are on pages 125–128.

Clinical research studies

Clinical research studies test how well different types of medical care work and if they're safe. Medicare covers some costs, like office visits and tests, in qualifying clinical research studies. You may pay 20% of the Medicare-approved amount, and the Part B deductible may apply.

Note: If you're in a Medicare Advantage Plan (like an HMO or PPO), some costs may be covered by Original Medicare and some may be covered by your Medicare Advantage Plan.

Colorectal cancer screenings

Medicare covers these screenings to help find precancerous growths or find cancer early, when treatment is most effective. One or more of these tests may be covered:

- **Multi-target stool DNA test**—This lab test is generally covered once every 3 years if you meet all of these conditions:
    - —Are between ages 50–85.
    - —Show no symptoms of colorectal disease including, but not limited to, lower gastrointestinal pain, blood in stool, positive guaiac fecal occult blood test or fecal immunochemical test.
    - —At average risk for developing colorectal cancer, meaning:
        - Have no personal history of adenomatous polyps, colorectal cancer, inflammatory bowel disease, including Crohn's Disease and ulcerative colitis.
        - Have no family history of colorectal cancer or adenomatous polyps, familial adenomatous polyposis, or hereditary nonpolyposis colorectal cancer.

You pay nothing for the test if the doctor or other qualified health care provider accepts assignment.

- **Screening fecal occult blood test**—This test is covered once every 12 months if you're 50 or older. You pay nothing for the test if the doctor or other qualified health care provider accepts assignment.

- **Screening flexible sigmoidoscopy**—This test is generally covered once every 48 months if you're 50 or older, or 120 months after a previous screening colonoscopy for those not at high risk. You pay nothing for the test if the doctor or other qualified health care provider accepts assignment.

- **Screening colonoscopy**—This test is generally covered once every 120 months (high risk every 24 months) or 48 months after a previous flexible sigmoidoscopy. There's no minimum age. You pay nothing for the test if the doctor or other qualified health care provider accepts assignment.
  Note: If a polyp or other tissue is found and removed during the colonoscopy, you may have to pay 20% of the Medicare-approved amount for the doctor's services and a copayment in a hospital outpatient setting. The Part B deductible doesn't apply.

- **Screening barium enema**—This test is generally covered once every 48 months if you're 50 or older (high risk every 24 months) when used instead of a sigmoidoscopy or colonoscopy. You pay 20% of the Medicare-approved amount for the doctor services. In a hospital outpatient setting, you also pay the hospital a copayment. The Part B deductible doesn't apply.

Continuous Positive Airway Pressure (CPAP) therapy

Medicare covers a 3-month trial of CPAP therapy if you've been diagnosed with obstructive sleep apnea. Medicare may cover it longer if you meet in person with your doctor, and your doctor documents in your medical record that the CPAP therapy is helping you.

You pay 20% of the Medicare-approved amount for rental of the machine and purchase of related supplies (like masks and tubing), and the Part B deductible applies. Medicare pays the supplier to rent the machine for 13 months if you've been using it without interruption. After you've rented the machine for 13 months, you own it.

Note: If you had a CPAP machine before you got Medicare, Medicare may cover rental or a replacement CPAP machine and/or CPAP accessories if you meet certain requirements.

If you live in certain areas of the country, you may have to use specific suppliers for Medicare to pay for a CPAP machine and/or accessories. See pages 45–46 for more information.

Definitions of blue words are on pages 125–128.

Defibrillator (implantable automatic)

Medicare covers these devices for some people diagnosed with heart failure. If the surgery takes place in an outpatient setting, you pay 20% of the Medicare-approved amount for the doctor's services. If you get the device as a hospital outpatient, you also pay the hospital a copayment. In most cases, the copayment amount can't be more than the Part A hospital stay deductible. The Part B deductible applies. Part A covers surgeries to implant defibrillators in a hospital inpatient setting. See Hospital care (inpatient care) on page 33–34.

Depression screening

Medicare covers one depression screening per year. The screening must be done in a primary care setting (like a doctor's office) that can provide follow-up treatment and referrals. You pay nothing for this screening if the doctor or other qualified health care provider accepts assignment.

Diabetes screenings

Medicare covers these screenings if your doctor determines you're at risk for diabetes. You may be eligible for up to 2 diabetes screenings each year. You pay nothing for the test if your doctor or other qualified health care provider accepts assignment.

Diabetes self-management training

Medicare covers diabetes outpatient self-management training to teach you to cope with and manage your diabetes. The program may include tips for eating healthy, being active, monitoring blood sugar, taking medication, and reducing risks. You must have diabetes and a written order from your doctor or other health care provider. You pay 20% of the Medicare-approved amount, and the Part B deductible applies.

Definitions of blue words are on pages 125–128.

Diabetes supplies

Medicare covers blood sugar testing monitors, blood sugar test strips, lancet devices and lancets, blood sugar control solutions, and therapeutic shoes (in some cases). Medicare only covers insulin if it's medically necessary and you use an external insulin pump to administer the insulin. You pay 20% of the Medicare-approved amount, and the Part B deductible applies.

Note: Medicare prescription drug coverage (Part D) may cover insulin, certain medical supplies used to inject insulin (like syringes), and some oral diabetic drugs. Check with your plan for more information.

Important! You may need to use specific suppliers for some types of diabetic testing supplies. Visit Medicare.gov/supplierdirectory to find a list of suppliers for your area.

Doctor and other health care provider services

Medicare covers medically necessary doctor services (including outpatient services and some doctor services you get when you're a hospital inpatient) and covered preventive services. Medicare also covers services provided by other health care providers, like physician assistants, nurse practitioners, social workers, physical therapists, and psychologists. Except for certain preventive services (for which you may pay nothing), you pay 20% of the Medicare-approved amount, and the Part B deductible applies.

Durable medical equipment (DME)

Medicare covers items like oxygen equipment and supplies, wheelchairs, walkers, and hospital beds ordered by a doctor or other health care provider enrolled in Medicare for use in the home. Some items must be rented. You pay 20% of the Medicare-approved amount, and the Part B deductible applies.

Make sure your doctors and DME suppliers are enrolled in Medicare. Doctors and suppliers have to meet strict standards to enroll and stay enrolled in Medicare. If your doctors or suppliers aren't enrolled, Medicare won't pay the claims they submit. It's also important to ask your suppliers if they participate in Medicare before you get DME. If suppliers are participating suppliers, they must accept assignment (that is, they're limited to charging you only coinsurance and the Part B deductible on the Medicare-approved amount). If suppliers are enrolled in Medicare but aren't "contract suppliers," they may choose not to accept assignment. If suppliers don't accept assignment, there's no limit on the amount they can charge you. To find suppliers who accept assignment, visit Medicare.gov/supplierdirectory or call 1-800-MEDICARE (1-800-633-4227). TTY users should call 1-877-486-2048. You can also call 1-800-MEDICARE if you're having problems with your DME supplier, or you need to file a complaint.

For more information, visit Medicare.gov/publications to view the booklet "Medicare Coverage of Durable Medical Equipment and Other Devices."

Durable Medical Equipment, Prosthetics, Orthotics, and Supplies (DMEPOS) Competitive Bidding Program: If you have Original Medicare and live in a Competitive Bidding Area (CBA) and use equipment or supplies included under the program (or get the items while visiting a CBA), you generally must use Medicare contract suppliers if you want Medicare to help pay for the item.

Visit Medicare.gov/supplierdirectory to see if you live in a CBA and to find Medicare-approved suppliers in your area. If your ZIP code is in a CBA, the items included in the program are marked with an orange star. You can also call 1-800-MEDICARE.

For more information visit Medicare.gov/publications to view the booklet "Your Guide to Medicare's Durable Medical Equipment Prosthetics, Orthotics, & Supplies (DMEPOS) Competitive Bidding Program."

EKG or ECG (electrocardiogram) screening

Medicare covers a one-time screening EKG/ECG if referred by your doctor or other health care provider as part of your one-time "Welcome to Medicare" preventive visit. See page 60. You pay 20% of the Medicare-approved amount, and the Part B deductible applies. An EKG/ECG is also covered as a diagnostic test. See page 58. If you have the test at a hospital or a hospital-owned clinic, you also pay the hospital a copayment.

Emergency department services

These services are covered when you have an injury, a sudden illness, or an illness that quickly gets much worse. You pay a specified copayment for the hospital emergency department visit, and you pay 20% of the Medicare-approved amount for the doctor's or other health care provider's services. The Part B deductible applies. However, your costs may be different if you're admitted to the hospital as an inpatient.

Eyeglasses (limited)

Medicare covers one pair of eyeglasses with standard frames (or one set of contact lenses) after cataract surgery that implants an intraocular lens. You pay 20% of the Medicare-approved amount, and the Part B deductible applies.

Note: Medicare will only pay for contact lenses or eyeglasses provided by a supplier enrolled in Medicare, no matter who submits the claim (you or your provider).

Federally Qualified Health Center (FQHC) services

FQHCs provide many outpatient primary care and preventive health services. There's no deductible, and generally, you're responsible for paying 20% of the charges or 20% of the Medicare-approved amount. You pay nothing for most preventive services. All FQHCs offer a sliding fee schedule to persons with incomes below 200% of the Federal poverty level. To find a FQHC near you, visit findahealthcenter.hrsa.gov.

Definitions of blue words are on pages 125–128.

Flu shots

Medicare generally covers one flu shot per flu season. You pay nothing for the flu shot if the doctor or other qualified health care provider accepts assignment for giving the shot.

Foot exams and treatment

Medicare covers foot exams and treatment if you have diabetes-related nerve damage and/or meet certain conditions. You pay 20% of the Medicare-approved amount, and the Part B deductible applies. In a hospital outpatient setting, you also pay the hospital a copayment.

Glaucoma tests

These tests are covered once every 12 months for people at high risk for the eye disease glaucoma. You're at high risk if you have diabetes, a family history of glaucoma, are African American and 50 or older, or are Hispanic and 65 or older. An eye doctor who's legally allowed by the state must do the tests. You pay 20% of the Medicare-approved amount, and the Part B deductible applies. In a hospital outpatient setting, you also pay the hospital a copayment.

Hearing and balance exams

Medicare covers these exams if your doctor or other health care provider orders them to see if you need medical treatment. You pay 20% of the Medicare-approved amount, and the Part B deductible applies. In a hospital outpatient setting, you also pay the hospital a copayment.

Note: Original Medicare doesn't cover hearing aids or exams for fitting hearing aids.

Hepatitis B shots

Medicare covers these shots for people at medium or high risk for Hepatitis B. Some risk factors include hemophilia, End-Stage Renal Disease (ESRD), diabetes, if you live with someone who has Hepatitis B, or if you're a health care worker and have frequent contact with blood or body fluids. Check with your doctor to see if you're at medium or high risk for Hepatitis B. You pay nothing for the shot if the doctor or other qualified health care provider accepts assignment.

Hepatitis C screening test

Medicare covers one Hepatitis C screening test if you meet one of these conditions:

- You're at high risk because you have a current or past history of illicit injection drug use.
- You had a blood transfusion before 1992.
- You were born between 1945–1965.

Medicare also covers yearly repeat screenings for certain people at high risk.

Medicare will only cover Hepatitis C screening tests if they're ordered by a primary care doctor or other primary care provider. You pay nothing for the screening test if the doctor or other qualified health care provider accepts assignment.

HIV screening

Medicare covers HIV (Human Immunodeficiency Virus) screenings once every 12 months for:

- People between the ages of 15–65.
- People younger than 15 and older than 65, who are at increased risk.

Note: Medicare also covers this test up to 3 times during a pregnancy.

Definitions of blue words are on pages 125–128.

You pay nothing for the HIV screening if the doctor or other qualified health care provider accepts assignment.

Home health services

You can use your home health benefits under Part A and/or Part B. Medicare covers medically necessary part-time or intermittent skilled nursing care, and/or physical therapy, speech-language pathology services, and/or services if you have a continuing need for occupational therapy. A doctor, or certain health care professionals who work with a doctor, must see you face-to-face before a doctor can certify that you need home health services. A doctor must order your care, and a Medicare-certified home health agency must provide it.

Home health services may also include medical social services, part-time or intermittent home health aide services, durable medical equipment, and medical supplies for use at home. You must be homebound, which means both of these are true:

1. You have trouble leaving your home without help (like using a cane, wheelchair, walker, or crutches; special transportation; or help from another person) because of an illness or injury.

2. Leaving your home isn't recommended because of your condition, and you're normally unable to leave your home because it's a major effort.

You pay nothing for covered home health services. You pay 20% of the Medicare-approved amount, and the Part B deductible applies, for Medicare-covered medical equipment.

Kidney dialysis services and supplies

Generally, Medicare covers 3 dialysis treatments per week if you have End-Stage Renal Disease (ESRD). This includes all ESRD-related drugs and biologicals, laboratory tests, home dialysis training, support services, equipment, and supplies. The dialysis facility is responsible for coordinating your dialysis services (at home or in a facility). You pay 20% of the Medicare-approved amount, and the Part B deductible applies.

Kidney disease education services

Medicare covers up to 6 sessions of kidney disease education services if you have Stage IV chronic kidney disease, and your doctor or other health care provider refers you for the service. You pay 20% of the Medicare-approved amount, and the Part B deductible applies.

Laboratory services

Medicare covers laboratory services including certain blood tests, urinalysis, certain tests on tissue specimens, and some screening tests. You generally pay nothing for these services.

Lung cancer screening

Medicare covers a lung cancer screening with Low Dose Computed Tomography (LDCT) once per year if you meet all of these conditions:

- You're 55–77.
- You're asymptomatic (you don't have signs or symptoms of lung cancer).
- You're either a current smoker or have quit smoking within the last 15 years.
- You have a tobacco smoking history of at least 30 "pack years" (an average of one pack a day for 30 years).
- You get a written order from a physician or qualified non-physician practitioner.

You generally pay nothing for this service if the primary care doctor or other qualified health care provider accepts assignment.

Note: Before your first lung cancer screening, you'll need to schedule an appointment with your doctor to discuss the benefits and risks of lung cancer screening. You and your doctor can decide whether lung cancer screening is right for you.

Medical nutrition therapy services

Medicare may cover medical nutrition therapy and certain related services if you have diabetes or kidney disease, or you have had a kidney transplant in the last 36 months, and your doctor or other health care provider refers you for the service. You pay nothing for these services if the doctor or other qualified health care provider accepts assignment.

Definitions of blue words are on pages 125–128.

Mental health care (outpatient)

Medicare covers mental health care services to help with conditions like depression or anxiety. Coverage includes services generally provided in an outpatient setting (like a doctor's or other health care provider's office or hospital outpatient department), including visits with a psychiatrist or other doctor, clinical psychologist, nurse practitioner, physician assistant, clinical nurse specialist, or clinical social worker. Laboratory tests are also covered. Certain limits and conditions may apply.

Generally, you pay 20% of the Medicare-approved amount and the Part B deductible applies for mental health care services.

Note: Inpatient mental health care is covered under Part A.

Obesity screening and counseling

If you have a body mass index (BMI) of 30 or more, Medicare covers face-to-face individual behavioral therapy sessions to help you lose weight. This counseling may be covered if you get it in a primary care setting (like a doctor's office), where it can be coordinated with your other care and a personalized prevention plan. You pay nothing for this service if the primary care doctor or other qualified primary care practitioner accepts assignment.

Occupational therapy

Medicare covers evaluation and treatment to help you perform activities of daily living (like dressing or bathing) when your doctor or other health care provider certifies you need it. There may be a limit on the amount Medicare will pay for these services in a single year, and there may be certain exceptions to these limits. You pay 20% of the Medicare-approved amount, and the Part B deductible applies.

Outpatient hospital services

Medicare covers many diagnostic and treatment services in hospital outpatient departments. Generally, you pay 20% of the Medicare-approved amount for the doctor's or other health care provider's services. You may pay more for services you get in a hospital outpatient setting than you'll pay for the same care in a doctor's office. In addition to the amount you pay the doctor, you'll also usually pay the hospital a copayment for each service you get in a hospital outpatient setting, except for certain preventive services that don't have a copayment. In most cases, the copayment can't be more than the Part A hospital stay deductible for each service. The Part B deductible applies, except for certain preventive services. If you get hospital outpatient services in a critical access hospital, your copayment may be higher and may exceed the Part A hospital stay deductible.

Outpatient medical and surgical services and supplies

Medicare covers approved procedures like X-rays, casts, stitches, or outpatient surgeries. You pay 20% of the Medicare-approved amount for the doctor's or other health care provider's services. You generally pay the hospital a copayment for each service you get in a hospital outpatient setting. In most cases, for each service provided, the copayment can't be more than the Part A hospital stay deductible. The Part B deductible applies, and you pay all costs for items or services that Medicare doesn't cover.

Physical therapy

Medicare covers evaluation and treatment for injuries and diseases that change your ability to function when your doctor or other health care provider certifies your need for it. There may be a limit on the amount Medicare will pay for these services in a single year, and there may be certain exceptions to these limits. You pay 20% of the Medicare-approved amount, and the Part B deductible applies.

Definitions of blue words are on pages 125–128.

Pneumococcal shot

Medicare covers a pneumococcal shot to help prevent pneumococcal infections (like certain types of pneumonia). Medicare also covers a different second shot if it's given one year (or later) after the first shot. Talk with your doctor or other health care provider to see if you need one or both of the pneumococcal shots. You pay nothing for these shots if the doctor or other qualified health care provider accepts assignment for giving the shot.

Prescription drugs (limited)

Medicare covers a limited number of drugs like injections you get in a doctor's office, certain oral anti-cancer drugs, drugs used with some types of durable medical equipment (like a nebulizer or external infusion pump), immunosuppressant drugs (see pages 58–59), and, under very limited circumstances, certain drugs you get in a hospital outpatient setting. You pay 20% of the Medicare-approved amount for these covered drugs, and the Part B deductible applies.

If the covered drugs you get in a hospital outpatient setting are part of your outpatient services, you pay a copayment for the services. However, other types of drugs in a hospital outpatient setting (sometimes called "self-administered drugs" or drugs you'd normally take on your own) aren't covered by Part B. What you pay depends on whether you have Part D or other prescription drug coverage, whether your drug plan covers the drug, and whether the hospital's pharmacy is in your drug plan's network. Contact your prescription drug plan to find out what you pay for drugs you get in a hospital outpatient setting that aren't covered under Part B.

Other than the examples above, you pay 100% for most prescription drugs, unless you have Part D or other drug coverage. See pages 85–96 for more information about Part D.

Prostate cancer screenings

Medicare covers a Prostate Specific Antigen (PSA) test and a digital rectal exam once every 12 months for men over 50 (beginning the day after your 50th birthday). You pay nothing for the PSA test. You pay 20% of the Medicare-approved amount, and the Part B deductible applies for the digital rectal exam. In a hospital outpatient setting, you also pay the hospital a copayment.

Prosthetic/orthotic items

Medicare covers arm, leg, back, and neck braces; artificial eyes; artificial limbs (and their replacement parts); some types of breast prostheses (after mastectomy); and prosthetic devices needed to replace an internal body part or function (including ostomy supplies, and parenteral and enteral nutrition therapy) when ordered by a doctor or other health care provider enrolled in Medicare.

For Medicare to cover your prosthetic or orthotic, you must go to a supplier that's enrolled in Medicare. You pay 20% of the Medicare-approved amount, and the Part B deductible applies.

Important! **DMEPOS Competitive Bidding Program:** To get enteral nutrition therapy in most areas of the country, you generally must use specific suppliers called "contract suppliers," or Medicare won't pay and you'll likely pay full price. See page 45–46 for more information.

Pulmonary rehabilitation

Medicare covers a comprehensive pulmonary rehabilitation program if you have moderate to very severe chronic obstructive pulmonary disease (COPD) and have a referral from the doctor treating this chronic respiratory disease. You pay 20% of the Medicare-approved amount if you get the service in a doctor's office. You also pay the hospital a copayment per session if you get the service in a hospital outpatient setting. The Part B deductible applies.

Rural Health Clinic (RHC) services

Definitions of blue words are on pages 125–128.

RHCs furnish many outpatient primary care and preventive health services. RHCs are located in non-urban areas that are in medically underserved or shortage areas. Generally, you're responsible for paying 20% of the charges, and the Part B deductible applies. You pay nothing for most preventive services.

Second surgical opinions

Medicare covers second surgical opinions for surgery that isn't an emergency. In some cases, Medicare covers third surgical opinions. You pay 20% of the Medicare-approved amount, and the Part B deductible applies.

Sexually transmitted infection (STI) screening and counseling

Medicare covers STI screenings for chlamydia, gonorrhea, syphilis, and Hepatitis B. These screenings are covered for people who are pregnant and for certain people who are at increased risk for an STI when the tests are ordered by a primary care doctor or other primary care practitioner. Medicare covers these tests once every 12 months or at certain times during pregnancy.

Medicare also covers up to 2 individual, 20–30 minute, face-to-face, high-intensity behavioral counseling sessions each year for sexually active adults at increased risk for STIs. Medicare will only cover these counseling sessions if they're provided by a primary care doctor or other primary care practitioner and take place in a primary care setting (like a doctor's office). Counseling conducted in an inpatient setting, like a skilled nursing facility, won't be covered as a preventive service.

You pay nothing for these services if the primary care doctor or other qualified primary care practitioner accepts assignment.

Shots

Part B covers:
- Flu shots. See page 48.
- Hepatitis B shots. See page 49.
- Pneumococcal shots. See page 54.

Note about the shingles shot:

The shingles shot isn't covered by Part A or Part B. Generally, Medicare prescription drug plans (Part D) cover all commercially available vaccines (like the shingles shot) needed to prevent illness. Contact your Medicare drug plan for more information about coverage.

Definitions of blue words are on pages 125–128.

Smoking and tobacco-use cessation (counseling to stop smoking or using tobacco products)

Medicare covers up to 8 face-to-face visits in a 12-month period. All people with Medicare who use tobacco are covered. You pay nothing for the counseling sessions if the doctor or other qualified health care provider accepts assignment.

Speech-language pathology services

Medicare covers evaluation and treatment to regain and strengthen speech and language skills, including cognitive and swallowing skills, when your doctor or other health care provider certifies you need it. There may be a limit on the amount Medicare will pay for these services in a single year, and there may be certain exceptions to these limits. You pay 20% of the Medicare-approved amount, and the Part B deductible applies.

Surgical dressing services

Medicare covers medically necessary treatment of a surgical or surgically treated wound. You pay 20% of the Medicare-approved amount for the doctor's or other health care provider's services. You pay a fixed copayment for these services when you get them in a hospital outpatient setting. The Part B deductible applies. You pay nothing for the supplies.

Telehealth

Medicare covers services like office visits, psychotherapy, consultations, and certain other medical or health services provided using an interactive, two-way telecommunications system (like real-time audio and video) by an eligible provider who isn't at your location. These services are available in rural areas, under certain conditions, but only if you're located at: a doctor's office, hospital, critical access hospital, Rural Health Clinic, Federally Qualified Health Center, hospital-based dialysis facility, skilled nursing facility, or community mental health center. For most of these services, you pay 20% of the Medicare-approved amount, and the Part B deductible applies.

Tests (other than lab tests)

Medicare covers X-rays, MRIs, CT scans, EKG/ECGs, and some other diagnostic tests. You pay 20% of the Medicare-approved amount, and the Part B deductible applies. If you get the test at a hospital as an outpatient, you also pay the hospital a copayment that may be more than 20% of the Medicare-approved amount, but, in most cases, this amount can't be more than the Part A hospital stay deductible. See Laboratory services on page 51 for other Part B-covered tests.

Transitional Care Management Services

Medicare may cover this service if you're returning to your community after a stay at certain facilities, like a hospital or skilled nursing facility. The health care provider who's managing your transition back into the community will work to coordinate and manage your care for the first 30 days after you return home. He or she will work with you and your family and caregiver(s), as appropriate, and with your other health care providers. You'll also be able to get an in-person office visit within 2 weeks of your return home. The health care provider may also review information on the care you received in the facility, provide information to help you transition back to living at home, work with other care providers, help you with referrals or arrangements for follow-up care or community resources, assist you with scheduling, and help you manage your medications. The Part B deductible and coinsurance apply.

Transplants and immunosuppressive drugs

Medicare covers doctor services for heart, lung, kidney, pancreas, intestine, and liver transplants under certain conditions but only in Medicare-certified facilities. Medicare also covers bone marrow and cornea transplants under certain conditions.

Note: The transplant surgery may be covered as a hospital inpatient service under Part A. See pages 33–34 for more information.

Medicare covers immunosuppressive drugs if the transplant was covered by Medicare or an employer or union group health plan was required to pay before Medicare paid for the transplant. You must have Part A at the time of the covered transplant, and you must have Part B at the time you get immunosuppressive drugs. You pay 20% of the Medicare-approved amount for the drugs, and the Part B deductible applies.

If you're thinking about joining a Medicare Advantage Plan (like an HMO or PPO) and are on a transplant waiting list or believe you need a transplant, check with the plan before you join to make sure your doctors, other health care providers, and hospitals are in the plan's network. Also, check the plan's coverage rules for prior authorization.

Note: Medicare drug plans (Part D) may cover immunosuppressive drugs if they aren't covered by Original Medicare.

Travel (health care needed when traveling outside the U.S.)

Medicare generally doesn't cover health care while you're traveling outside the U.S. (The "U.S." includes the 50 states, the District of Columbia, Puerto Rico, the U.S. Virgin Islands, Guam, the Northern Mariana Islands, and American Samoa.) There are some exceptions, including cases where Medicare may pay for services you get while on board a ship within the territorial waters adjoining the land areas of the U.S. Medicare may pay for inpatient hospital, doctor, or ambulance services you get in a foreign country in these rare cases:

- You're in the U.S. when an emergency occurs, and the foreign hospital is closer than the nearest U.S. hospital that can treat your medical condition.
- You're traveling through Canada without unreasonable delay by the most direct route between Alaska and another U.S. state when a medical emergency occurs, and the Canadian hospital is closer than the nearest U.S. hospital that can treat the emergency.
- You live in the U.S. and the foreign hospital is closer to your home than the nearest U.S. hospital that can treat your medical condition, regardless of whether an emergency exists.

Medicare may cover medically necessary ambulance transportation to a foreign hospital only with admission for medically necessary covered inpatient hospital services. You pay 20% of the Medicare-approved amount, and the Part B deductible applies.

Definitions of blue words are on pages 125–128.

Urgently needed care

Medicare covers urgently needed care to treat a sudden illness or injury that isn't a medical emergency. You pay 20% of the Medicare-approved amount for the doctor's or other health care provider's services, and the Part B deductible applies. In a hospital outpatient setting, you also pay the hospital a copayment.

"Welcome to Medicare" preventive visit

During the first 12 months that you have Part B, you can get a "Welcome to Medicare" preventive visit. This visit includes a review of your medical and social history related to your health, and education and counseling about preventive services, including certain screenings, shots, and referrals for other care, if needed. When you make your appointment, let your doctor's office know that you'd like to schedule your "Welcome to Medicare" preventive visit. You pay nothing for the "Welcome to Medicare" preventive visit if the doctor or other qualified health care provider accepts assignment.

If your doctor or other health care provider performs additional tests or services during the same visit that aren't covered under this preventive benefit, you may have to pay coinsurance, and the Part B deductible may apply.

Yearly "Wellness" visit

If you've had Part B for longer than 12 months, you can get a yearly "Wellness" visit to develop or update a personalized plan to prevent disease or disability based on your current health and risk factors. This visit is covered once every 12 months.

Your provider will ask you to fill out a questionnaire, called a "Health Risk Assessment," as part of this visit. Answering these questions can help you and your provider develop a personalized prevention plan to help you stay healthy and get the most out of your visit. When you make your appointment, let your doctor's office know that you'd like to schedule your yearly "Wellness" visit.

Note: Your first yearly "Wellness" visit can't take place within 12 months of your enrollment in Part B or your "Welcome to Medicare" preventive visit. However, you don't need to have had a "Welcome to Medicare" preventive visit to qualify for a yearly "Wellness" visit.

You pay nothing for the yearly "Wellness" visit if the doctor or other qualified health care provider accepts assignment.

If your doctor or other health care provider performs additional tests or services during the same visit that aren't covered under this preventive benefit, you may have to pay coinsurance, and the Part B deductible may apply.

What's NOT covered by Part A and Part B?

Medicare doesn't cover everything. If you need certain services that aren't covered under Medicare Part A or Part B, you'll have to pay for them yourself unless:
- You have other coverage (including Medicaid) to cover the costs.
- You're in a Medicare health plan that covers these services.

Even if Medicare covers a service or item, you generally have to pay deductibles, coinsurance, and/or copayments.

Some of the items and services that Medicare doesn't cover include:
- ✗ Most dental care.
- ✗ Eye examinations related to prescribing glasses.
- ✗ Dentures.
- ✗ Cosmetic surgery.
- ✗ Acupuncture.
- ✗ Hearing aids and exams for fitting them.
- ✗ Long-term care. See next page for more information about paying for long-term care.
- ✗ Concierge care (also called concierge medicine, retainer-based medicine, boutique medicine, platinum practice, or direct care).

Definitions of blue words are on pages 125–128.

Paying for long-term care

Long-term care includes non-medical care for people who have a chronic illness or disability. This includes non-skilled personal care assistance, like help with everyday activities, including dressing, bathing, and using the bathroom. **Medicare and most health insurance plans, including Medicare Supplement Insurance (Medigap) policies, don't pay for this type of care, sometimes**

called "custodial care." You may be eligible for this type of care through Medicaid, or you can choose to buy private long-term care insurance. Long-term care can be provided at home, in the community, in an assisted living facility, or in a nursing home. It's important to start planning for long-term care now to maintain your independence and to make sure you get the care you may need, in the setting you want, in the future.

Long-term care resources

Use these resources to get more information about long-term care:

- Visit longtermcare.gov to learn more about planning for long-term care.

- Call your State Insurance Department to get information about long-term care insurance. Visit Medicare.gov/contacts, or call 1-800-MEDICARE (1-800-633-4227) to get the phone number. TTY users should call 1-877-486-2048.

- Call your State Health Insurance Assistance Program (SHIP). See page 121 for the phone number.

- Call the National Association of Insurance Commissioners at 1-866-470-6242 to get a copy of "A Shopper's Guide to Long-Term Care Insurance."

- Visit the Eldercare Locator, a public service of the U.S. Administration on Aging, at eldercare.gov to find help in your community.

Definitions of blue words are on pages 125–128.

Section 4 —

What's Original Medicare?

How does Original Medicare work?

Original Medicare is one of your health coverage choices as part of Medicare. You'll have Original Medicare unless you choose a Medicare Advantage Plan (like an HMO or PPO).

Original Medicare is coverage managed by the federal government. You generally have to pay a portion of the cost for each service covered by Original Medicare. See the next page for the general rules about how it works.

Original Medicare

Can I get my health care from any doctor, other health care provider, or hospital?	In most cases, yes. You can go to any doctor, other health care provider, hospital, or other facility that's enrolled in Medicare and accepting Medicare patients. Visit Medicare.gov to search for and compare health care providers, hospitals, and facilities in your area.
Are prescription drugs covered?	No, with a few exceptions (see pages 33, 54, and 58), most prescriptions aren't covered. You can add drug coverage by joining a Medicare Prescription Drug Plan (Part D). See pages 85–96.
Do I need to choose a primary care doctor?	No.
Do I have to get a referral to see a specialist?	In most cases, no, but the specialist must be enrolled in Medicare.
Should I get a supplemental policy?	You may already have employer or union coverage that may pay costs that Original Medicare doesn't. If not, you may want to buy a Medicare Supplement Insurance (Medigap) policy if you're eligible. See pages 81–84.
What else do I need to know about Original Medicare?	■ You generally pay a set amount for your health care (deductible) before Medicare pays its share. Then, Medicare pays its share, and you pay your share (coinsurance/copayment) for covered services and supplies. There's no yearly limit for what you pay out-of-pocket. ■ You usually pay a monthly premium for Part B. See pages 99–100 for information about help paying your Part B premium. ■ You generally don't need to file Medicare claims. The law requires providers (like doctors, hospitals, skilled nursing facilities, and home health agencies) and suppliers to file your claims for the covered services and supplies you get.

What do I pay?

Your out-of-pocket costs in Original Medicare depend on:

- Whether you have Part A and/or Part B. Most people have both.
- Whether your doctor, other health care provider, or supplier accepts "assignment."
- The type of health care you need and how often you need it.
- Whether you choose to get services or supplies Medicare doesn't cover. If you do, you pay all costs unless you have other insurance that covers it.
- Whether you have other health insurance that works with Medicare.
- Whether you have Medicaid or get help from your state paying your Medicare costs.
- Whether you have a Medicare Supplement Insurance (Medigap) policy.
- Whether you and your doctor or other health care provider sign a private contract. See page 66.

How do I know what Medicare paid?

If you have Original Medicare, you'll get a "Medicare Summary Notice" (MSN) in the mail every 3 months that lists all the services billed to Medicare. The MSN shows what Medicare paid and what you may owe the provider. The MSN isn't a bill. Review your MSNs to be sure you got all the services, supplies, or equipment listed.

If you need to change your address on your notice, call Social Security at 1-800-772-1213. TTY users should call 1-800-325-0778. If you get Railroad Retirement Board (RRB) benefits, call the RRB at 1-877-772-5772. TTY users should call 1-312-751-4701.

Important!

Get your Medicare Summary Notices electronically

Go paperless and get your "Medicare Summary Notices" electronically (also called "eMSNs"). You can sign up by visiting MyMedicare.gov. If you sign up for eMSNs, we'll send you an email each month when they're available in your MyMedicare.gov account. The eMSNs contain the same information as paper MSNs. You won't get printed copies of your MSNs in the mail if you choose eMSNs.

Definitions of blue words are on pages 125–128.

What's assignment?

Assignment means that your doctor, provider, or supplier agrees (or is required by law) to accept the Medicare-approved amount as full payment for covered services.

Important!

To find out if your doctors and other health care providers accept assignment or participate in Medicare, visit Medicare.gov/physician or Medicare.gov/supplier. You can also call 1-800-MEDICARE (1-800-633-4227), or ask your doctor, provider, or supplier. TTY users should call 1-877-486-2048. If your doctor, provider, or supplier accepts assignment:

- Your out-of-pocket costs may be less.
- They agree to charge you only the Medicare deductible and coinsurance amount and usually wait for Medicare to pay its share before asking you to pay your share.
- They have to submit your claim directly to Medicare and can't charge you for submitting the claim.

Non-participating providers haven't signed an agreement to accept assignment for all Medicare-covered services, but they can still choose to accept assignment for individual services. These providers are called "non-participating." Here's what happens if your doctor, provider, or supplier doesn't accept assignment:

- **You might have to pay the entire charge at the time of service.** Your doctor, provider, or supplier is supposed to submit a claim to Medicare for any Medicare-covered services they provide to you. If they don't submit the Medicare claim once you ask them to, call 1-800-MEDICARE.
- **They can charge you more than the Medicare-approved amount, but there's a limit called "the limiting charge."** Call 1-800-MEDICARE to find out if you were charged the right amount.

What are private contracts?

A "private contract" is a written agreement between you and a doctor or other health care provider who has decided **not** to provide services to anyone through Medicare. The private contract only applies to the services provided by the doctor or other provider who asked you to sign it.

Section 5 —

Learn about Medicare Advantage Plans (Part C) & Other Medicare Health Plans

What are Medicare Advantage Plans?

A Medicare Advantage Plan (like an HMO or PPO) is another way to get your Medicare coverage. Medicare Advantage Plans, sometimes called "Part C" or "MA Plans," are offered by Medicare-approved private companies that must follow rules set by Medicare. If you join a Medicare Advantage Plan, you'll still have Medicare but you'll get your Medicare Part A (Hospital Insurance) and Medicare Part B (Medical Insurance) coverage from the Medicare Advantage Plan, not Original Medicare. You'll generally get your services from a plan's network of providers. Remember, in most cases, you must use the card from your Medicare Advantage Plan to get your Medicare-covered services. Keep your Medicare card in a safe place because you'll need it if you ever switch back to Original Medicare.

Medicare Advantage Plans cover all Medicare Part A and Part B services

In all types of Medicare Advantage Plans, you're always covered for emergency and urgent care. Medicare Advantage Plans must cover all of the services that Original Medicare covers. However, Original Medicare covers hospice care, some new Medicare benefits, and some costs for clinical research studies, even if you're in a Medicare Advantage Plan.

Medicare Advantage Plans may offer extra coverage, like vision, hearing, dental, and other health and wellness programs. Most include Medicare prescription drug coverage (Part D). In addition to your Part B premium, you might have to pay a monthly premium for the Medicare Advantage Plan.

Definitions of blue words are on pages 125–128.

Section 5

Medicare Advantage Plans must follow Medicare's rules

Medicare pays a fixed amount for your coverage each month to the companies offering Medicare Advantage Plans. These companies must follow rules set by Medicare. However, each Medicare Advantage Plan can charge different out-of-pocket costs and have different rules for how you get services (like whether you need a referral to see a specialist or if you have to go to doctors, facilities, or suppliers that belong to the plan's network for non-emergency or non-urgent care). These rules can change each year. The plan must notify you about any changes before the start of the next enrollment year. Remember, you have the option each year during Open Enrollment to keep your current plan, choose a different plan, or switch to Original Medicare.

Important!

Read the information you get from your plan

If you're in a Medicare Advantage Plan, review the "Evidence of Coverage" (EOC) and "Annual Notice of Change" (ANOC) your plan sends you each year. The EOC gives you details about what the plan covers, how much you pay, and more. The ANOC includes any changes in coverage, costs, provider networks, service area, and more that will be effective in January. If you don't get these important documents before the start of Open Enrollment, contact your plan.

What are the different types of Medicare Advantage Plans?

- **Health Maintenance Organization (HMO) plans**—See page 73.
- **Preferred Provider Organization (PPO) plans**—See page 74.
- **Private Fee-for-Service (PFFS) plans**—See page 75.
- **Special Needs Plans (SNPs)**—See page 76.
- **HMO Point-of-Service (HMOPOS) plans**—These are HMO plans that may allow you to get some services out-of-network for a higher copayment or coinsurance.

- **Medical Savings Account (MSA) plans**—These plans combine a high-deductible health plan with a bank account. Medicare deposits money into the account (usually less than the deductible). You can use the money to pay for your health care services during the year. MSA plans don't offer Medicare drug coverage. If you want drug coverage, you have to join a Medicare Prescription Drug Plan.

What else should I know about Medicare Advantage Plans?

- You have Medicare rights and protections, including the right to appeal. See pages 104–107.
- You can check with the plan before you get a service to find out if it's covered and what your costs may be.
- You must follow plan rules. It's important to check with the plan for information about your rights and responsibilities.
- If you go to a doctor, other health care provider, facility, or supplier that doesn't belong to the plan's network for non-emergency or non-urgent care services, your services may not be covered, or your costs could be higher. In most cases, this applies to Medicare Advantage HMOs and PPOs.
- Providers can join or leave a plan's provider network anytime during the year. Your plan can also change the providers in the network anytime during the year. If this happens, you may need to choose a new provider.
- If you join a clinical research study, some costs may be covered by Original Medicare and some may be covered by your Medicare Advantage Plan.
- Medicare Advantage Plans can't charge more than Original Medicare for certain services, like chemotherapy, dialysis, and skilled nursing facility care.
- Medicare Advantage Plans have a yearly limit on your out-of-pocket costs for medical services. Once you reach this limit, you'll pay nothing for covered services. This limit may be different between Medicare Advantage Plans and can change each year. You should consider this when choosing a plan.

Definitions of blue words are on pages 125–128.

Joining and leaving

- You can join a Medicare Advantage Plan even if you have a pre-existing condition, except for End-Stage Renal Disease (ESRD), for which there are special rules. See page 71.

- **You can only join or leave a Medicare Advantage Plan at certain times during the year.** See pages 77–78.

- Each year, Medicare Advantage Plans can choose to leave Medicare or make changes to the services they cover and what you pay. If the plan decides to stop participating in Medicare, you'll have to join another Medicare Advantage Plan or return to Original Medicare. See page 104.

- Medicare Advantage Plans must follow certain rules when giving you information about how to join their plan. See page 113 for more information about these rules and how to protect your personal information.

Prescription drug coverage

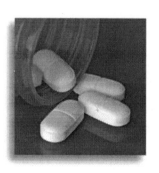

You usually get prescription drug coverage (Part D) through the Medicare Advantage Plan. In certain types of plans that can't offer drug coverage (like MSA plans) or choose not to offer (like some PFFS plans) drug coverage, you can join a Medicare Prescription Drug Plan. **If your Medicare Advantage Plan includes prescription drug coverage and you join a Medicare Prescription Drug Plan, you'll be disenrolled from your Medicare Advantage Plan and returned to Original Medicare.**

Who can join?

You must meet these conditions to join a Medicare Advantage Plan:

- You have Part A and Part B.
- You live in the plan's service area.
- You don't have End-Stage Renal Disease (ESRD), except as explained on page 71.
- You're a U.S. citizen or lawfully present in the United States.

Definitions of blue words are on pages 125–128.

What if I have other coverage?

Talk to your employer, union, or other benefits administrator about their rules before you join a Medicare Advantage Plan. In some cases,  joining a Medicare Advantage Plan might cause you to lose your employer or union coverage. If you lose coverage for yourself, you may also lose coverage for your spouse and dependents. In other cases, if you join a Medicare Advantage Plan, you may still be able to use your employer or union coverage along with the plan you join. **Remember, if you drop your employer or union coverage, you may not be able to get it back.**

What if I have a Medicare Supplement Insurance (Medigap) Policy?

You can't use (and can't be sold) a Medicare Supplement Insurance (Medigap) policy while you're in a Medicare Advantage Plan. You can't use it to pay for any expenses (copayments, deductibles, and premiums) you have under a Medicare Advantage Plan. If you already have a Medigap policy and join a Medicare Advantage Plan, you'll probably want to drop your Medigap policy. **If you drop your Medigap policy, you may not be able to get it back.** See page 83.

What if I have End-Stage Renal Disease (ESRD)?

If you have End-Stage Renal Disease (ESRD), you can only join a Medicare Advantage Plan in certain situations:

- If you're already in a Medicare Advantage Plan when you develop ESRD, you can stay in your plan or you may be able to join another Medicare Advantage Plan offered by the same company.
- If you're in a Medicare Advantage Plan, and the plan leaves Medicare or no longer provides coverage in your area, you have a one-time right to join another Medicare Advantage Plan.
- If you have an employer or union health plan or other health coverage through a company that offers one or more Medicare Advantage Plan(s), you may be able to join one of that company's Medicare Advantage Plans.
- If you've had a successful kidney transplant, you may be able to join a Medicare Advantage Plan.
- You may be able to join a Medicare Special Needs Plan (SNP) that covers people with ESRD if one is available in your area.

For more information visit Medicare.gov/publications to view the booklet "Medicare Coverage of Kidney Dialysis & Kidney Transplant Services."

Note: If you have ESRD and Original Medicare, you may join a Medicare Prescription Drug Plan.

What do I pay?

Your out-of-pocket costs in a Medicare Advantage Plan depend on:

- Whether the plan charges a monthly premium in addition to your monthly Part B premium.
- Whether the plan pays any of your monthly Part B (or Part A if you have to buy it) premium.
- Whether the plan has a yearly deductible or any additional deductibles for certain services.
- How much you pay for each visit or service (copayments or coinsurance).
- The type of health care services you need and how often you get them.
- Whether you go to a doctor or supplier who accepts assignment (if you're in a Preferred Provider Organization, Private Fee-for-Service Plan, or Medical Savings Account Plan and you go out-of-network). See page 66 for more information about assignment.
- Whether you get services from a network provider or a provider that doesn't contract with the plan.
- Whether you need extra benefits and if the plan charges for them.
- The plan's yearly limit on your out-of-pocket costs for all medical services. Once you reach this limit, you'll pay nothing for covered services.
- Whether you have Medicaid or get help from your state.

To learn more about your costs in specific Medicare Advantage Plans, visit Medicare.gov/find-a-plan.

Types of Medicare Advantage Plans

HMO

Health Maintenance Organization (HMO) plan

Can I get my health care from any doctor, other health care provider, or hospital?

No. You generally must get your care and services from doctors, other health care providers, or hospitals in the plan's network (except emergency care, out-of-area urgent care, or out-of-area dialysis). In some plans, you may be able to go out-of-network for certain services, usually for a higher cost. This is called an HMO with a point-of-service (POS) option.

Are prescription drugs covered?

In most cases, yes. If you want Medicare drug coverage, you must join an HMO plan that offers prescription drug coverage. Check with the plan for more information.

Do I need to choose a primary care doctor?

In most cases, yes. Check with the plan for more information.

Do I have to get a referral to see a specialist?

In most cases, yes. Certain services, like yearly screening mammograms, don't require a referral. Check with the plan for more information.

What else do I need to know about this type of plan?

- If your doctor or other health care provider leaves the plan's network, your plan will notify you. You may choose another doctor in the plan's network.
- If you get health care outside the plan's network, you may have to pay the full cost.
- It's important that you follow the plan's rules, like getting prior approval for a certain service when needed.

Definitions of blue words are on pages 125–128.

Preferred Provider Organization (PPO) plan

Can I get my health care from any doctor, other health care provider, or hospital?

In most cases, yes. PPOs have network doctors, other health care providers, and hospitals, but you can also use out-of-network providers for covered services, usually for a higher cost. Check with the plan for more information.

Are prescription drugs covered?

In most cases, yes. If you want Medicare drug coverage, you must join a PPO plan that offers prescription drug coverage. Check with the plan for more information.

Do I need to choose a primary care doctor?

No.

Do I have to get a referral to see a specialist?

In most cases, no. Check with the plan for more information.

What else do I need to know about this type of plan?

- PPO plans aren't the same as Original Medicare or Medigap.
- Medicare PPO plans usually offer more benefits than Original Medicare, but you may have to pay extra for these benefits.

Definitions
of blue words
are on pages
125–128.

Private Fee-for-Service (PFFS) plan

Can I get my health care from any doctor, other health care provider, or hospital?

You can go to any Medicare-approved doctor, other health care provider, or hospital that accepts the plan's payment terms and agrees to treat you. Not all providers will. If you join a PFFS plan that has a network, you can also see any of the network providers who've agreed to always treat plan members. You can also choose an out-of-network doctor, hospital, or other provider, who accepts the plan's terms, but you may pay more. Check with the plan for more information.

Are prescription drugs covered?

Sometimes. If your PFFS plan doesn't offer drug coverage, you can join a Medicare Prescription Drug Plan (Part D) to get coverage. Check with the plan for more information.

Do I need to choose a primary care doctor?

No.

Do I have to get a referral to see a specialist?

No.

What else do I need to know about this type of plan?

- PFFS plans aren't the same as Original Medicare or Medigap.
- The plan decides how much you must pay for services.
- Some PFFS plans contract with a network of providers who agree to always treat you, even if you've never seen them before.
- Out-of-network doctors, hospitals, and other providers may decide not to treat you, even if you've seen them before.
- For each service you get, make sure your doctors, hospitals, and other providers agree to treat you under the plan and accept the plan's payment terms.
- In an emergency, doctors, hospitals, and other providers must treat you.

Special Needs Plan (SNP)

Can I get my health care from any doctor, other health care provider, or hospital?

You generally must get your care and services from doctors, other health care providers, or hospitals in the plan's network (except emergency care, out-of-area urgent care, or out-of-area dialysis). Check with the plan for more information.

Are prescription drugs covered?

Yes. All SNPs must provide Medicare prescription drug coverage (Part D).

Do I need to choose a primary care doctor?

Generally, yes. Check with the plan for more information.

Do I have to get a referral to see a specialist?

In most cases, yes. Certain services, like yearly screening mammograms, don't require a referral. Check with the plan for more information.

What else do I need to know about this type of plan?

- A plan must limit membership to these groups: 1) people who live in certain institutions (like nursing homes) or who require nursing care at home, or 2) people who are eligible for both Medicare and Medicaid, or 3) people who have specific chronic or disabling conditions (like diabetes, End-Stage Renal Disease, HIV/AIDS, chronic heart failure, or dementia). Plans may further limit membership.

- Plans will coordinate the services and providers you need to help you stay healthy and follow doctors' or other health care providers' orders.

- Visit Medicare.gov/find-a-plan to see if there are SNPs available in your area.

Definitions of blue words are on pages 125–128.

When can I join, switch, or drop a Medicare Advantage Plan?

- When you first become eligible for Medicare, you can sign up during your Initial Enrollment Period. See page 23.
- If you have Part A coverage and you get Part B for the first time during the General Enrollment Period, you can also join a Medicare Advantage Plan. See page 24.
- Between October 15–December 7, anyone with Medicare can join, switch, or drop a Medicare Advantage Plan. Your coverage will begin on January 1, as long as the plan gets your request by December 7.

Can I make changes to my coverage after December 7?

Between January 1–February 14, if you're in a Medicare Advantage Plan, you can leave that plan and switch to Original Medicare. If you switch to Original Medicare during this period, you'll have until February 14 to also join a Medicare Prescription Drug Plan to add drug coverage. Your coverage will begin the first day of the month after the plan gets your enrollment request. During this period, you **can't**:

- Switch from Original Medicare to a Medicare Advantage Plan.
- Switch from one Medicare Advantage Plan to another.
- Switch from one Medicare Prescription Drug Plan to another.
- Join, switch, or drop a Medicare Medical Savings Account Plan.

Special Enrollment Periods

In most cases, you must stay enrolled for the calendar year starting the date your coverage begins. However, in certain situations, you may be able to join, switch, or drop a Medicare Advantage Plan during a Special Enrollment Period. Some examples are:

- You move out of your plan's service area.
- You have Medicaid.
- You qualify for Extra Help. See pages 97–99.
- You live in an institution (like a nursing home).

5-Star Special Enrollment Period

You can switch to a Medicare Advantage Plan or Medicare Cost Plan (see page 79) that has **5 stars for its overall star rating** from December 8, 2016–November 30, 2017. You can only use this Special Enrollment Period once during this timeframe. The overall star ratings are available at Medicare.gov/find-a-plan.

Important! ▶ You may lose your prescription drug coverage if you move from a Medicare Advantage Plan that has drug coverage to a 5-star Medicare Advantage Plan that doesn't. You'll have to wait until the next Open Enrollment Period to get drug coverage, and you may have to pay a late enrollment penalty. See pages 90–92.

How do I switch?

Follow these steps if you're already in a Medicare Advantage Plan and want to switch:

- **To switch to a new Medicare Advantage Plan,** simply join the plan you choose during one of the enrollment periods explained on pages 77–78. You'll be disenrolled automatically from your old plan when your new plan's coverage begins.

- **To switch to Original Medicare,** contact your current plan, or call 1-800-MEDICARE (1-800-633-4227). TTY users should call 1-877-486-2048. If you don't have drug coverage, you should consider joining a Medicare Prescription Drug Plan. You may also want to consider joining a Medicare Supplement Insurance (Medigap) policy if you're eligible. See page 81 for more information about buying a Medigap policy.

For more information on joining, dropping, and switching plans, visit Medicare.gov or call 1-800-MEDICARE.

Definitions of blue words are on pages 125–128.

Are there other types of Medicare health plans?

Some types of Medicare health plans that provide health care coverage aren't Medicare Advantage Plans but are still part of Medicare. Some of these plans provide Medicare Part A (Hospital Insurance) and Medicare Part B (Medical Insurance) coverage, while others provide only Part B coverage. In addition, some also provide Part D prescription drug coverage. These plans have some of the same rules as Medicare Advantage Plans. However, each type of plan has special rules and exceptions, so you should contact any plans you're interested in to get more details.

Medicare Cost Plans

Medicare Cost Plans are a type of Medicare health plan available in certain areas of the country. Here's what you should know about Medicare Cost Plans:

- You can join even if you only have Part B.
- If you have Part A and Part B and go to a non-network provider, the services are covered under Original Medicare. You'd pay the Part A and Part B coinsurance and deductibles.
- You can join anytime the Cost Plan is accepting new members.
- You can leave anytime and return to Original Medicare.
- You can either get your Medicare prescription drug coverage from the Cost Plan (if offered), or you can join a Medicare Prescription Drug Plan. Even if the Cost Plan offers prescription drug coverage, you can choose to get drug coverage from a different plan.

Note: You can add or drop Medicare prescription drug coverage only at certain times. See pages 86–87.

For more information about Medicare Cost Plans, visit the Medicare Plan Finder at Medicare.gov/find-a-plan. Your State Health Insurance Assistance Program (SHIP) can also give you more information. See page 121 for the phone number.

Programs of All-inclusive Care for the Elderly (PACE)

PACE is a Medicare and Medicaid program offered in many states that allows people who otherwise need a nursing home-level of care to remain in the community. To qualify for PACE, you must meet these conditions:

- You're 55 or older.
- You live in the service area of a PACE organization.
- You're certified by your state as needing a nursing home-level of care.
- At the time you join, you're able to live safely in the community with the help of PACE services.

PACE provides coverage for many services, including prescription drugs, doctor or other health care practitioner visits, transportation, home care, hospital visits, and even nursing home stays whenever necessary.

If you have Medicaid, you won't have to pay a monthly premium for the long-term care portion of the PACE benefit. If you have Medicare but not Medicaid, you'll be charged a monthly premium to cover the long-term care portion of the PACE benefit and a premium for Medicare Part D drugs. However, in PACE, there's never a deductible or copayment for any drug, service, or care approved by the PACE team of health care professionals.

Contact your Medicaid office to find out if you qualify for a PACE program near you. Visit Medicare.gov/contacts, or call 1-800-MEDICARE (1-800-633-4227) to get the phone number. TTY users should call 1-877-486-2048.

Medicare Innovation Projects

Medicare develops innovative models, demonstrations, and pilot projects to test and measure the effect of potential changes in Medicare. These projects help to find new ways to improve health care quality and reduce costs. Usually, they operate only a limited time for a specific group of people and/or are offered only in specific areas. To learn more about the current Medicare models, demonstrations, and pilot projects, visit innovation.cms.gov. You can also call 1-800-MEDICARE.

Definitions of blue words are on pages 125–128.

Section 6 —

What are Medicare Supplement Insurance (Medigap) Policies?

Original Medicare pays for many, but not all, health care services and supplies. Medicare Supplement Insurance policies, sold by private companies, can help pay some of the health care costs that Original Medicare doesn't cover, like copayments, coinsurance, and deductibles. **Medicare Supplement Insurance policies are also called Medigap policies.**

Some Medigap policies also offer coverage for services that Original Medicare doesn't cover, like medical care when you travel outside the U.S. Generally, Medigap policies don't cover long-term care (like care in a nursing home), vision or dental care, hearing aids, eyeglasses, or private-duty nursing.

Medigap policies are standardized

Every Medigap policy must follow federal and state laws designed to protect you, and they must be clearly identified as "Medicare Supplement Insurance." Insurance companies can sell you only a "standardized" policy identified in most states by letters A through D, F through G, and K through N. All policies offer the same basic benefits, but some offer additional benefits so you can choose which one meets your needs. In Massachusetts, Minnesota, and Wisconsin, Medigap policies are standardized in a different way.

How do I compare Medigap policies?

The chart below shows basic information about the different benefits that Medigap policies cover. If a percentage appears, the Medigap plan covers that percentage of the benefit, and you're responsible for the rest.

Benefits	Medicare Supplement Insurance (Medigap) plans									
	A	**B**	**C**	**D**	**F***	**G**	**K**	**L**	**M**	**N**
Medicare Part A coinsurance and hospital costs (up to an additional 365 days after Medicare benefits are used)	100%	100%	100%	100%	100%	100%	100%	100%	100%	100%
Medicare Part B coinsurance or copayment	100%	100%	100%	100%	100%	100%	50%	75%	100%	100% **
Blood (first 3 pints)	100%	100%	100%	100%	100%	100%	50%	75%	100%	100%
Part A hospice care coinsurance or copayment	100%	100%	100%	100%	100%	100%	50%	75%	100%	100%
Skilled nursing facility care coinsurance			100%	100%	100%	100%	50%	75%	100%	100%
Part A deductible		100%	100%	100%	100%	100%	50%	75%	50%	100%
Part B deductible			100%		100%					
Part B excess charges					100%	100%				
Foreign travel emergency (up to plan limits)			80%	80%	80%	80%			80%	80%
							Out-of-pocket limit in 2016			
							$4,960	$2,480		

* Plan F also offers a high-deductible plan in some states. If you choose this option, this means you must pay for Medicare-covered costs (coinsurance, copayments, and deductibles) up to the deductible amount of $2,180 in 2016 before your policy pays anything.

** Plan N pays 100% of the Part B coinsurance, except for a copayment of up to $20 for some office visits and up to a $50 copayment for emergency room visits that don't result in an inpatient admission.

What else should I know about Medicare Supplement Insurance (Medigap)?

Important facts

- You must have Part A and Part B.

- You pay the private insurance company a monthly premium for your Medigap policy in addition to your monthly Part B premium that you pay to Medicare. Contact the company to find out how to pay your premium.

- A Medigap policy only covers one person. Spouses must buy separate policies.

- You can't have prescription drug coverage in both your Medigap policy and a Medicare drug plan. See page 95.

- It's important to compare Medigap policies since the costs can vary and may go up as you get older. Some states limit Medigap premium costs.

When to buy

- The best time to buy a Medigap policy is during your Medigap Open Enrollment Period. This 6-month period begins on the first day of the month in which you're 65 or older **and** enrolled in Part B. (Some states have additional Open Enrollment Periods.) After this enrollment period, you may not be able to buy a Medigap policy. If you're able to buy one, it may cost more.

- If you delay enrolling in Part B because you have group health coverage based on your (or your spouse's) current employment, your Medigap Open Enrollment Period won't start until you sign up for Part B.

- Federal law generally doesn't require insurance companies to sell Medigap policies to people under 65. If you're under 65, you might not be able to buy the Medigap policy you want, or any Medigap policy, until you turn 65. However, some states require Medigap insurance companies to sell Medigap policies to people under 65.

Definitions
of blue words
are on pages
125–128.

How does Medigap work with Medicare Advantage Plans?

- If you have a Medicare Advantage Plan (like an HMO or PPO), it's illegal for anyone to sell you a Medigap policy unless you're switching back to Original Medicare. If you're not planning to leave your Medicare Advantage Plan, and someone tries to sell you a Medigap policy, report it to your State Insurance Department.

- If you have a Medigap policy and join a Medicare Advantage Plan, you may want to drop your Medigap policy. Your Medigap policy **can't** be used to pay your Medicare Advantage Plan copayments, deductibles, and premiums. If you want to cancel your Medigap policy, contact your insurance company. In most cases, if you drop your Medigap policy to join a Medicare Advantage Plan, you won't be able to get it back.

- If you join a Medicare Advantage Plan for the first time, and you aren't happy with the plan, you'll have special rights to buy a Medigap policy if you return to Original Medicare within 12 months of joining.

  —If you had a Medigap policy before you joined, you may be able to get the same policy back if the company still sells it. If it isn't available, you can buy another Medigap policy.

  —If you joined a Medicare Advantage Plan when you were first eligible for Medicare, you can choose from any Medigap policy within the first year of joining.

  —The Medigap policy can no longer have prescription drug coverage, even if you had it before, but you may be able to join a Medicare Prescription Drug Plan.

Where can I get more information?

- Visit Medicare.gov to find policies in your area.

- Visit Medicare.gov/publications to view the booklet "Choosing a Medigap Policy: A Guide to Health Insurance for People with Medicare."

- Call your State Insurance Department. Visit Medicare.gov/contacts, or call 1-800-MEDICARE (1-800-633-4227) to get the phone number. TTY users should call 1-877-486-2048.

- Call your State Health Insurance Assistance Program (SHIP). See page 121 for the phone number.

Definitions of blue words are on pages 125–128.

Section 7 —

Get Information about Prescription Drug Coverage (Part D)

How does Medicare prescription drug coverage (Part D) work?

Medicare offers prescription drug coverage to everyone with Medicare. Even if you don't take many prescriptions now, you should consider joining a Medicare drug plan. If you decide not to join a Medicare drug plan when you're first eligible, and you don't have other creditable prescription drug coverage or get Extra Help, you'll likely pay a late enrollment penalty if you join a plan later. Generally, you'll pay this penalty for as long as you have Medicare prescription drug coverage. See pages 90–92. To get Medicare prescription drug coverage, you must join a plan approved by Medicare to offer Medicare drug coverage. Each plan can vary in cost and specific drugs covered.

There are 2 ways to get Medicare prescription drug coverage:

1. **Medicare Prescription Drug Plans.** These plans (sometimes called "PDPs") add drug coverage to Original Medicare, some Medicare Cost Plans, some Medicare Private Fee-for-Service (PFFS) plans, and Medicare Medical Savings Account (MSA) plans. You must have Part A **and/or** Part B to join a Medicare Prescription Drug Plan.

2. **Medicare Advantage Plans (like HMOs or PPOs) or other** Medicare health plans **that offer Medicare prescription drug coverage.** You get all of your Part A, Part B, and prescription drug coverage (Part D), through these plans. Medicare Advantage Plans with prescription drug coverage are sometimes called "MA-PDs." Remember, you must have Part A **and** Part B to join a Medicare Advantage Plan, and not all of these plans offer drug coverage.

In either case, you must live in the service area of the Medicare drug plan you want to join. **Both types of plans are called "Medicare drug plans" in this handbook.**

Important!

If you have employer or union coverage

Call your benefits administrator before you make any changes, or sign up for any other coverage. If you drop your employer or union coverage, you may not be able to get it back. You also may not be able to drop your employer or union **drug** coverage without also dropping your employer or union **health** (doctor and hospital) coverage. If you drop coverage for yourself, you may also have to drop coverage for your spouse and dependents. If you want to know how Medicare prescription drug coverage works with other drug coverage you may have, see pages 94–96.

When can I join, switch, or drop a Medicare drug plan?

- When you first become eligible for Medicare, you can join during your Initial Enrollment Period. See page 23.
- If you get Part B for the first time during the General Enrollment Period, you can also join a Medicare drug plan. See page 24.
- During Open Enrollment, between October 15–December 7 each year. Your coverage begins on January 1 of the following year, as long as the plan gets your request during Open Enrollment.
- At any time if you qualify for Extra Help. See pages 97–99.

Definitions of blue words are on pages 125–128.

Special Enrollment Periods

You generally must stay enrolled for the calendar year. However, in certain situations, you may be able to join, switch, or drop Medicare drug plans at other times. Some examples are if you:

- Move out of your plan's service area.
- Lose other creditable prescription drug coverage.
- Live in an institution (like a nursing home).
- Have Medicaid.
- Qualify for Extra Help. See pages 97–99.

5-Star Special Enrollment Period

You can switch to a Medicare Prescription Drug Plan that has **5 stars for its overall star rating** from December 8, 2016 – November 30, 2017. You can only use this Special Enrollment Period once during this timeframe. The overall star ratings are available at Medicare.gov/find-a-plan.

Important!

If you have a Medicare Advantage Plan

If your Medicare Advantage Plan includes prescription drug coverage and you join a Medicare Prescription Drug Plan, you'll be disenrolled from your Medicare Advantage Plan and returned to Original Medicare.

How do I switch?

You can switch to a new Medicare drug plan simply by joining another drug plan during one of the times listed on pages 86–87. **You don't need to cancel your old Medicare drug plan.** Your old Medicare drug plan coverage will end when your new drug plan coverage begins. You should get a letter from your new Medicare drug plan telling you when your coverage with the new plan begins.

How do I drop a Medicare drug plan?

If you want to drop your Medicare drug plan and don't want to join a new plan, you can only do so during certain times. See pages 86–87. You can disenroll by calling 1-800-MEDICARE (1-800-633-4227). TTY users should call 1-877-486-2048. You can also send a letter to the plan to tell them you want to disenroll. If you drop your plan and want to join another Medicare drug plan later, you have to wait for an enrollment period. You may have to pay a late enrollment penalty if you don't have creditable prescription drug coverage. See pages 90–92.

How much do I pay?

Below and continued on the next page are descriptions of what you pay in your Medicare drug plan. **Your actual drug plan costs will vary depending on:**

- Your prescriptions and whether they're on your plan's formulary (list of covered drugs) and depending on what "tier" the drug is in. See page 92.
- The plan you choose. Remember, plan costs can change each year.
- Which pharmacy you use (whether it offers preferred or standard cost sharing, is out-of-network, or is mail order).
- Whether you get Extra Help paying your Part D costs. See pages 97–99.

Monthly premium

Most drug plans charge a monthly fee that varies by plan. You pay this in addition to the Part B premium. If you're in a Medicare Advantage Plan (like an HMO or PPO) or a Medicare Cost Plan that includes Medicare prescription drug coverage, the monthly premium may include an amount for prescription drug coverage.

Note: Contact your drug plan (not Social Security or the Railroad Retirement Board (RRB)) if you want your premium deducted from your monthly Social Security or RRB payment. If you want to stop premium deductions and get billed directly, contact your drug plan.

Important!

If you have a higher income, you might pay more for your Part D coverage. If your income is above a certain limit ($85,000 if you file individually or $170,000 if you're married and file jointly), you'll pay an extra amount in addition to your plan premium (sometimes called "Part D-IRMAA"). This doesn't affect everyone, so most people won't have to pay a higher amount.

Usually, the extra amount will be deducted from your Social Security check. If you get benefits from the Railroad Retirement Board (RRB), the extra amount will be deducted from your RRB check. **If you're billed the amount by Medicare or the RRB, you must pay the extra amount to Medicare or the RRB and not your plan.** If you don't pay the extra amount, you could lose your Part D coverage. You may not be able to enroll in another plan right away and you may have to pay a late enrollment penalty for as long as you have Part D.

Definitions of blue words are on pages 125–128.

If you have to pay an extra amount and you disagree (for example, you have a life event that lowers your income), visit socialsecurity.gov or call Social Security at 1-800-772-1213. TTY users should call 1-800-325-0778.

Yearly deductible

This is the amount you must pay before your drug plan begins to pay its share of your covered drugs. Some drug plans don't have a deductible.

Copayments or coinsurance

These are the amounts you pay for your covered prescriptions after the deductible (if the plan has one). You pay your share and your drug plan pays its share for covered drugs. These amounts may vary.

Coverage gap

Most Medicare drug plans have a coverage gap (also called the "donut hole"). The coverage gap begins after you and your drug plan together have spent a certain amount for covered drugs. In 2017, once you enter the coverage gap, you pay 40% of the plan's cost for covered brand-name drugs and 51% of the plan's cost for covered generic drugs until you reach the end of the coverage gap. Not everyone will enter the coverage gap because their drug costs won't be high enough.

These costs (sometimes called true out-of-pocket, or "TrOOP," costs) all **count** toward you getting out of the coverage gap:

- Your yearly deductible, coinsurance, and copayments
- The discount you get on covered brand-name drugs in the coverage gap
- What you pay in the coverage gap

The drug plan premium and what you pay for drugs that aren't covered **don't count** toward getting you out of the coverage gap.

Some plans offer additional cost sharing reductions in the gap beyond the standard benefits and discounts on brand-name and generic drugs, but they may charge a higher monthly premium. Check with the plan first to see if your drugs would have additional cost-sharing reductions during the gap.

Catastrophic coverage

Once you get out of the coverage gap, you automatically get "catastrophic coverage." With catastrophic coverage, you only pay a coinsurance amount or copayment for covered drugs for the rest of the year.

Note: If you get Extra Help, you won't have some of these costs. See pages 97–99.

Important!

You can visit the Medicare Plan Finder at Medicare.gov/find-a-plan to compare the cost of plans in your area. For help comparing plan costs, contact your State Health Insurance Assistance Program (SHIP). See page 121 for the phone number.

What's the Part D late enrollment penalty?

The late enrollment penalty is an amount that's added to your Part D premium. You may owe a late enrollment penalty if at any time after your Initial Enrollment Period is over, there's a period of 63 or more days in a row when you don't have Part D or other creditable prescription drug coverage. You'll generally have to pay the penalty for as long as you have Part D coverage.

Note: If you get Extra Help, you don't pay a late enrollment penalty.

3 ways to avoid paying a penalty:

1. **Join a Medicare drug plan when you're first eligible.** Even if you don't take many prescriptions now, you should consider joining a Medicare drug plan to avoid a penalty. You may be able to find a plan that meets your needs with little to no monthly premiums.

2. **Don't go 63 days or more in a row without a Medicare drug plan or other creditable coverage.** Creditable prescription drug coverage could include drug coverage from a current or former employer or union, TRICARE, Indian Health Service, the Department of Veterans Affairs, or health coverage. Your plan must tell you each year if your drug coverage is creditable coverage.

Definitions of blue words are on pages 125–128.

3. **Tell your plan about any drug coverage you had if they ask about it.** If you don't tell the plan about your creditable prescription drug coverage, you may have to pay a penalty for as long as you have Part D coverage.

How much more will I pay?

The cost of the late enrollment penalty depends on how long you didn't have creditable prescription drug coverage. Currently, the late enrollment penalty is calculated by multiplying 1% of the "national base beneficiary premium" ($34.10 in 2016) by the number of full, uncovered months that you were eligible but didn't join a Medicare drug plan and went without other creditable prescription drug coverage. The final amount is rounded to the nearest $.10 and added to your monthly premium. Since the "national base beneficiary premium" may increase each year, the penalty amount may also increase each year. After you join a Medicare drug plan, the plan will tell you if you owe a penalty and what your premium will be.

Example:
Mrs. Martin didn't join when she was first eligible—by June 2013. She doesn't have prescription drug coverage from any other source. She joined a Medicare drug plan during the 2015 Open Enrollment Period, and her coverage began on January 1, 2016.

Since Mrs. Martin was without creditable prescription drug coverage from July 2013–December 2015, her penalty in 2016 is 30% (1% for each of the 30 months) of $34.10 (the national base beneficiary premium for 2016), which is $10.23. The monthly penalty is rounded to the nearest $.10, so she'll be charged $10.20 each month in addition to her plan's monthly premium in 2016. She'll continue to pay a penalty for as long as she has Part D coverage, and the amount may go up each year.

Here's the math:

.30 (30% penalty) × **$34.10** (2016 base beneficiary premium) = **$10.23**

$10.23 (rounded to the nearest $0.10) = **$10.20**

$10.20 = Mrs. Martin's monthly late enrollment penalty for 2016

What if I don't agree with the penalty?

If you disagree with your penalty, you can ask for a review or reconsideration. You'll need to fill out a reconsideration request form (that your Medicare drug plan will send you) by the date listed in the letter. You can provide proof that supports your case, like information about previous creditable prescription drug coverage.

If you need help, call your plan.

Which drugs are covered?

Information about a plan's list of covered drugs (called a "formulary") isn't included in this handbook because each plan has its own formulary. Many Medicare drug plans place drugs into different "tiers" on their formularies. Drugs in each tier have a different

cost. For example, a drug in a lower tier will generally cost you less than a drug in a higher tier. In some cases, if your drug is in a higher tier and your prescriber (your doctor or other health care provider who's legally allowed to write prescriptions) thinks you need that drug instead of a similar drug in a lower tier, you or your prescriber can ask your plan for an exception to get a lower copayment for the drug in the higher tier. See pages 106–107 for more information on exceptions.

Contact the plan for its current formulary, or visit the plan's website. You can also visit the Medicare Plan Finder at Medicare.gov/find-a-plan, or call 1-800-MEDICARE (1-800-633-4227). TTY users should call 1-877-486-2048. Your plan will notify you of any formulary changes.

Important!

Definitions of blue words are on pages 125–128.

Each month that you fill a prescription, your drug plan mails you an "Explanation of Benefits" (EOB) notice. Review your notice and check it for mistakes. Contact your plan if you have questions or find mistakes. If you suspect fraud, call the Medicare Drug Integrity Contractor (MEDIC) at 1-877-7SAFERX (1-877-772-3379). See page 113 for more information about the MEDIC.

Plans may have these coverage rules:

- **Prior authorization**—You and/or your prescriber must contact the drug plan before you can fill certain prescriptions. Your prescriber may need to show that the drug is medically necessary for the plan to cover it.

- **Quantity limits**—Limits on how much medication you can get at a time.

- **Step therapy**—You must try one or more similar, lower-cost drugs before the plan will cover the prescribed drug.

If you or your prescriber believe that one of these coverage rules should be waived, you can ask for an exception. See pages 106–107.

Important!

Starting in 2017, almost all prescribers need to be enrolled in Medicare or have an "opt-out" request on file with Medicare for your prescriptions to be covered by your Medicare drug plan. If your prescriber isn't enrolled and hasn't "opted-out," you'll still be able to get a 3-month provisional fill of your prescription. This will give your prescriber time to enroll, or you time to find a new prescriber who's enrolled or has opted out. Contact your plan or your prescribers for more information.

Do you get automatic prescription refills in the mail?

Some people with Medicare get their prescription drugs by using an "automatic refill" service that automatically delivers prescription

drugs when they're about to run out. To make sure you still need a prescription before they send you a refill, prescription drug plans should get your approval to deliver a new or refilled prescription before each delivery, except when you ask for the refill or new prescription. If you get a prescription automatically by mail that you don't want, and you weren't contacted to see if you wanted it before it shipped, you may be eligible for a refund.

Medication Therapy Management (MTM) Program

If you're in a Medicare drug plan and take medications for different medical conditions, you may be eligible to get services, at no cost to you, through a MTM program. This program helps you understand your medications and use them safely. A pharmacist or other health professional will give you a comprehensive review of all your medications and talk with you about:

- How to get the most benefit from the drugs you take
- Any concerns you have, like medication costs and drug reactions
- How best to take your medications
- Any questions or problems you have about your prescription and over-the-counter medication

Visit Medicare.gov/find-a-plan to get general information about program eligibility for your Medicare drug plan or for other plans that interest you. Contact each drug plan for specific details.

How do other insurance and programs work with Part D?

The charts on this page and the next 2 pages provide information about how other insurance you have works with, or is affected by, Medicare prescription drug coverage (Part D).

Employer or union health coverage—Health coverage from your, your spouse's, or other family member's current or former employer or union. If you have prescription drug coverage based on your current or previous employment, your employer or union will notify you each year to let you know if your prescription drug coverage is creditable. **Keep the information you get.** Call your benefits administrator for more information before making any changes to your coverage.

Note: If you join a Medicare drug plan, you, your spouse, or your dependents may lose your employer or union health coverage.

Definitions of blue words are on pages 125–128.

COBRA—This is a federal law that may allow you to temporarily keep employer or union health coverage after the employment ends or after you lose coverage as a dependent of the covered employee. As explained on pages 24–25, there may be reasons why you should take Part B instead of, or in addition to, COBRA coverage. However, if you take COBRA and it includes creditable prescription drug coverage, you'll have a Special Enrollment Period to join a Medicare drug plan without paying a penalty when the COBRA coverage ends. Talk with your State Health Insurance Assistance Program (SHIP) to see if COBRA is a good choice for you. See page 121 for the phone number.

Medicare Supplement Insurance (Medigap) policy with prescription drug coverage—You may choose to join a Medicare drug plan because most Medigap drug coverage isn't creditable, and you may pay more if you join a drug plan later. See pages 90–92. Medigap policies can no longer be sold with prescription drug coverage, but if you have drug coverage under a current Medigap policy, you can keep it. If you join a Medicare drug plan, tell your Medigap insurance company so they can remove the prescription drug coverage under your Medigap policy and adjust your premiums. Call your Medigap insurance company for more information.

Note: Keep any creditable prescription drug coverage information you get from your plan. You may need it if you decide to join a Medicare drug plan later. Don't send creditable coverage letters or certificates to Medicare.

How does other government insurance work with Part D?

These types of insurance are all considered creditable prescription drug coverage, and in most cases, it will be to your advantage to keep this coverage if you have it.

Federal Employee Health Benefits (FEHB) Program—This is health coverage for current and retired federal employees and covered family members. FEHB plans usually include prescription drug coverage, so you don't need to join a Medicare drug plan. However, if you decide to join a Medicare drug plan, you can keep your FEHB plan, and in most cases, the Medicare plan will pay first. For more information for retirees, visit opm.gov/healthcare-insurance/healthcare, or call the Office of Personnel Management at 1-888-767-6738. TTY users should call 1-800-878-5707. If you're an active federal employee, you should contact your Benefits Officer. Visit apps.opm.gov/abo for a list of Benefits Officers. You can also call your plan if you have questions.

Veterans' benefits—This is health coverage for veterans and people who have served in the U.S. military. You may be able to get prescription drug coverage through the U.S. Department of Veterans Affairs (VA) program. You may join a Medicare drug plan, but if you do, you can't use both types of coverage for the same prescription at the same time. For more information, visit va.gov, or call the VA at 1-800-827-1000. TTY users should call 1-800-829-4833.

TRICARE (military health benefits)—This is a health care plan for active-duty service members, military retirees, and their families. **Most people with TRICARE who are entitled to Part A must have Part B to keep TRICARE prescription drug benefits**. If you have TRICARE, you don't need to join a Medicare Prescription Drug Plan. However, if you do, your Medicare drug plan pays first, and TRICARE pays second.

If you join a Medicare Advantage Plan (like an HMO or PPO) with prescription drug coverage, your Medicare Advantage Plan and TRICARE may coordinate their benefits if your Medicare Advantage Plan network pharmacy is also a TRICARE network pharmacy. Otherwise, you can file your own claim to get paid back for your out-of-pocket expenses. For more information, visit tricare.mil, or call the TRICARE Pharmacy Program at 1-877-363-1303. TTY users should call 1-877-540-6261.

Indian Health Service (IHS)—The IHS is the primary health care provider to the American Indian/Alaska Native (AI/AN) Medicare population. The Indian health care system, consisting of tribal, urban, and federally operated IHS health programs, delivers a spectrum of clinical and preventive health services through a network of hospitals, clinics, and other entities. Many Indian health facilities participate in the Medicare prescription drug program. If you get prescription drugs through an Indian health facility, you'll continue to get drugs at no cost to you, and your coverage won't be interrupted. Joining a Medicare drug plan may help your Indian health facility because the drug plan pays the Indian health facility for the cost of your prescriptions. Talk to your local Indian health benefits coordinator who can help you choose a plan that meets your needs and tell you how Medicare works with the Indian health care system.

Note: If you're getting care through an IHS or tribal health facility or program without being charged, you can continue to do so for some or all of your care. Getting Medicare doesn't affect your ability to get services through the IHS and tribal health facilities.

Section 8 —

Get Help Paying Your Health & Prescription Drug Costs

What if I need help paying my Medicare prescription drug costs?

If you have limited income and resources, you may qualify for help to pay for some health care and prescription drug costs.

Note: Extra Help isn't available in Puerto Rico, the U.S. Virgin Islands, Guam, the Northern Mariana Islands, or American Samoa. See page 102 for information about programs that are available in those areas.

Extra Help is a Medicare program to help people with limited income and resources pay Medicare prescription drug costs. You may qualify for Extra Help if your yearly income and resources are below these limits in 2016:

- Single person—income less than $17,820 and resources less than $13,640 per year
- Married person living with a spouse and no other dependents—income less than $24,030 and resources less than $27,250 per year

These amounts may change in 2017. You may qualify even if you have a higher income (like if you still work, live in Alaska or Hawaii, or have dependents living with you). Resources include money in a checking or savings account, stocks, bonds, mutual funds, and Individual Retirement Accounts (IRAs). Resources **don't** include your home, car, household items, burial plot, up to $1,500 for burial expenses (per person), or life insurance policies.

Definitions of blue words are on pages 125–128.

If you qualify for Extra Help and join a Medicare drug plan, you'll:

- Get help paying your Medicare drug plan's costs.
- Have no coverage gap.
- Have no late enrollment penalty.
- Have the chance to switch plans at any time. Any change you make will take effect the first day of the following month.

You automatically qualify for Extra Help if you have Medicare and meet any of these conditions:

- You have full Medicaid coverage.
- You get help from your state Medicaid program paying your Part B premiums (in a Medicare Savings Program). See pages 99–100.
- You get Supplemental Security Income (SSI) benefits.

To let you know you automatically qualify for Extra Help, Medicare will mail you a purple letter that you should keep for your records. You don't need to apply for Extra Help if you get this letter.

- If you aren't already in a Medicare drug plan, you must join one to use this Extra Help.
- If you don't join a Medicare drug plan, Medicare may enroll you in one so that you'll be able to use the Extra Help. If Medicare enrolls you in a plan, you'll get a yellow or green letter letting you know when your coverage begins.
- Different plans cover different drugs. Check to see if the plan you're enrolled in covers the drugs you use and if you can go to the pharmacies you want. Visit Medicare.gov/find-a-plan, or call 1-800-MEDICARE (1-800-633-4227) to compare with other plans in your area. TTY users should call 1-877-486-2048.
- If you have Medicaid and live in certain institutions (like a nursing home) or get home- and community-based services, you pay nothing for your covered prescription drugs.

If you don't want to join a Medicare drug plan (for example, because you want only your employer or union coverage), call the plan listed in your letter, or call 1-800-MEDICARE. Tell them you don't want to be in a Medicare drug plan (you want to "opt out"). If you continue to qualify for Extra Help or if your employer or union coverage is creditable prescription drug coverage, you won't have to pay a penalty if you join later.

Important! If you have employer or union coverage and you join a Medicare drug plan, you may lose your employer or union coverage even if you qualify for Extra Help. Call your employer's benefits administrator before you join a Medicare drug plan.

If you didn't automatically qualify for Extra Help, you can apply at anytime:

- Visit socialsecurity.gov/i1020 to apply online.
- Call Social Security at 1-800-772-1213. TTY users should call 1-800-325-0778.
- Visit your Medicaid office. Visit Medicare.gov/contacts, or call 1-800-MEDICARE (1-800-633-4227) to get the phone number. TTY users should call 1-877-486-2048.

Drug costs in 2017 for people who qualify will be no more than $3.30 for each generic drug and $8.25 for each brand-name drug. Look on the Extra Help letters you get, or contact your plan to find out your exact costs.

To get answers to your questions about Extra Help and help choosing a drug plan, call your State Health Insurance Assistance Program (SHIP). See page 121 for the phone number. You can also call 1-800-MEDICARE.

What if I need help paying my Medicare health care costs?

Medicare Savings Programs

If you have limited income and resources, you may be able to get help from your state to pay your Medicare costs if you meet certain conditions.

There are 4 kinds of Medicare Savings Programs:

1. **Qualified Medicare Beneficiary (QMB) Program**—If you're eligible, the QMB Program helps pay for Part A and/or Part B premiums. In addition, Medicare providers aren't allowed to bill you for Medicare deductibles, coinsurance, and copayments when you get services and items Medicare covers, except outpatient prescription drugs. Pharmacists may charge you up to a limited amount (no more than $3.70 in 2017) for prescription drugs covered by Medicare Part D. (If you have QMB, you automatically get Extra Help. See page 97.) To make sure your provider knows you have QMB, show both your Medicare and Medicaid or QMB card each time you get care. If you get a bill for medical care Medicare covers, call your provider or plan about the charges. Tell them that you have QMB and can't be charged for Medicare deductibles, coinsurance and copayments. If this doesn't resolve the billing problem, call 1-800-MEDICARE.

Definitions of blue words are on pages 125–128.

2. **Specified Low-Income Medicare Beneficiary (SLMB) Program—** Helps pay Part B premiums only.

3. **Qualifying Individual (QI) Program—**Helps pay Part B premiums only. You must apply each year for QI benefits and the applications are granted on a first-come first-served basis.

4. **Qualified Disabled and Working Individuals (QDWI) Program—** Helps pay Part A premiums only. You may qualify for this program if you have a disability and are working.

Important! The names of these programs and how they work may vary by state. Medicare Savings Programs aren't available in Puerto Rico and the U.S. Virgin Islands.

How do I qualify?
In most cases, to qualify for a Medicare Savings Program, you must have:
- Part A
- Monthly income less than $1,010 and resources less than $7,280—single person
- Monthly income less than $1,355 and resources less than $10,930— married and living together

Note: The amounts above are for 2016 and may change each year. Many states figure your income and resources differently, so you may qualify in your state even if your income or resources are higher than the amounts listed above. If you have income from working, you may qualify for benefits even if your income is higher than the limits above.

For more information
- Call or visit your Medicaid office, and ask for information on Medicare Savings Programs. To get the phone number for your state, visit Medicare.gov/contacts. You can also call 1-800-MEDICARE (1-800-633-4227), and say "Medicaid." TTY users should call 1-877-486-2048.
- Contact your State Health Insurance Assistance Program (SHIP). See page 121 for the phone number.

Definitions of blue words are on pages 125–128.

Medicaid
Medicaid is a joint federal and state program that helps pay medical costs if you have limited income and resources and meet other requirements. Some people qualify for both Medicare and Medicaid and are called **"dual eligibles."**

What does Medicaid cover?

- If you have Medicare and full Medicaid coverage, most of your health care costs are covered. You can get your Medicare coverage through Original Medicare or a Medicare Advantage Plan (like an HMO or PPO).
- If you have Medicare and full Medicaid coverage, Medicare covers your Part D prescription drugs. Medicaid may still cover some drugs and other care that Medicare doesn't cover.
- People with Medicaid may get coverage for services that Medicare may not or may partially cover, like nursing home care, personal care, and home- and community-based services.

How do I qualify?

- Medicaid programs vary from state to state. They may also have different names, like "Medical Assistance" or "Medi-Cal."
- Each state has different income and resource requirements.
- Many states have expanded their Medicaid programs to cover more people. Even if you were told you didn't qualify for Medicaid in the past, you may qualify under the new rules.
- In some states, you may need to be enrolled in Medicare, if eligible, to get Medicaid.
- Call your Medicaid office for more information and to see if you qualify. Visit Medicare.gov/contacts, or call 1-800-MEDICARE (1-800-633-4227) and say "Medicaid" to get the phone number. TTY users should call 1-877-486-2048.

Demonstration plans for people who have both Medicare and Medicaid

Medicare is working with several states and health plans to create demonstration plans for certain people who have both Medicare and Medicaid, called Medicare-Medicaid Plans. If you're interested in joining a Medicare-Medicaid Plan, visit Medicare.gov/find-a-plan to see if one is available in your area and if you qualify. Call your Medicaid office for more information.

State Pharmacy Assistance Programs (SPAPs)

Many states have SPAPs that help certain people pay for prescription drugs based on financial need, age, or medical condition. To find out if there's an SPAP in your state and how it works, call your State Health Insurance Assistance Program (SHIP). See page 121 for the phone number.

Pharmaceutical Assistance Programs (also called Patient Assistance Programs)

Many major drug manufacturers offer assistance programs for people with Medicare drug coverage who meet certain requirements. Visit Medicare.gov/pharmaceutical-assistance-program to learn more about Pharmaceutical Assistance Programs.

Programs of All-inclusive Care for the Elderly (PACE)

PACE is a Medicare and Medicaid program offered in many states that allows people who need a nursing home-level of care to remain in the community. See page 80 for more information.

Supplemental Security Income (SSI) benefits

SSI is a cash benefit paid by Social Security to people with limited income and resources who are disabled, blind, or 65 or older. SSI benefits aren't the same as Social Security benefits.

You can visit benefits.gov/ssa, and use the "Benefit Eligibility Screening Tool" to find out if you're eligible for SSI or other benefits. Call Social Security at 1-800-772-1213 or contact your local Social Security office for more information. TTY users should call 1-800-325-0778.

Note: People who live in Puerto Rico, the U.S. Virgin Islands, Guam, or American Samoa can't get SSI.

Programs for people who live in the U.S. territories

There are programs in Puerto Rico, the U.S. Virgin Islands, Guam, the Northern Mariana Islands, and American Samoa to help people with limited income and resources pay their Medicare costs. Programs vary in these areas. Call your Medicaid office to learn more, or call 1-800-MEDICARE (1-800-633-4227) and say "Medicaid" for more information. TTY users should call 1-877-486-2048.

Definitions of blue words are on pages 125–128.

Section 9 —

Know Your Rights & Protect Yourself from Fraud

What are my Medicare rights?

No matter how you get your Medicare, you have certain rights and protections. All people with Medicare have the right to:

- Be treated with dignity and respect at all times
- Be protected from discrimination
- Have their personal and health information kept private
- Get information in a language and format that they understand from Medicare, health care providers, and Medicare contractors
- Have questions about Medicare answered
- Have access to doctors, other health care providers, specialists, and hospitals
- Learn about their treatment choices in clear language that they can understand, and participate in treatment decisions
- Get Medicare-covered services in an emergency
- Get a decision about health care payment, coverage of services, or prescription drug coverage
- Request a review (appeal) of certain decisions about health care payment, coverage of services, or prescription drug coverage
- File complaints (sometimes called "grievances"), including complaints about the quality of their care

What are my rights if my plan stops participating in Medicare?

Medicare health and prescription drug plans can decide not to participate in Medicare for the coming year. In these cases, your coverage under the plan will end after December 31.

- You can choose another plan during Medicare Open Enrollment between October 15–December 7. Your coverage will begin January 1.
- **You'll also have a special right to join another** Medicare plan **until February 28, 2017.**

Your plan will send you a letter about your options before Open Enrollment.

What's an appeal?

An appeal is the action you can take if you disagree with a coverage or payment decision by Medicare or your Medicare plan. For example, you can appeal if Medicare or your plan denies:

- A request for a health care service, supply, item, or prescription drug that you think you should be able to get.
- A request for payment of a health care service, supply, item, or prescription drug you already got.
- A request to change the amount you must pay for a health care service, supply, item, or prescription drug.

You can also appeal if Medicare or your plan stops providing or paying for all or part of a health care service, supply, item, or prescription drug you think you still need.

If you decide to file an appeal, you can ask your doctor, supplier, or other health care provider for any information that may help your case. Keep a copy of everything you send to Medicare or your plan as part of your appeal.

How do I file an appeal?

How you file an appeal depends on the type of Medicare coverage you have:

If you have Original Medicare

1. Get the "Medicare Summary Notice" (MSN) that shows the item or service you're appealing. See page 65.

2. Circle the item(s) you disagree with on the MSN, and write an explanation of why you disagree with the decision on the MSN or on a separate piece of paper and attach it to the MSN.

3. Include your name, phone number, and Medicare number on the MSN, and sign it. Keep a copy for your records.

4. Send the MSN, or a copy, to the company that handles bills for Medicare (Medicare Administrative Contractor) listed on the MSN. You can include any other additional information you have about your appeal. Or, you can use CMS Form 20027. To view or print this form, visit CMS.gov/cmsforms/downloads/cms20027.pdf, or call 1-800-MEDICARE (1-800-633-4227) to have a copy mailed to you. TTY users should call 1-877-486-2048.

5. You must file the appeal within 120 days of the date you get the MSN in the mail.

You'll generally get a decision from the Medicare Administrative Contractor within 60 days after they get your request. If Medicare will cover the item(s) or service(s), it will be listed on your next MSN.

If you have a Medicare health plan

Learn how to file an appeal by looking at the materials your plan sends you, calling your plan, or visiting Medicare.gov/appeals.

In some cases, you can file a fast appeal. See materials from your plan and page 107.

Definitions of blue words are on pages 125–128.

If you have a Medicare Prescription Drug Plan

You have the right to do all of these (even before you buy a certain drug):

- Get a written explanation (called a "coverage determination") from your Medicare drug plan. A coverage determination is the first decision made by your Medicare drug plan (not the pharmacy) about your benefits, including whether a certain drug is covered, whether you've met the requirements to get a requested drug, how much you pay for a drug, and whether to make an exception to a plan rule when you request it.

- Ask for an exception if you or your prescriber (your doctor or other health care provider who's legally allowed to write prescriptions) believes you need a drug that isn't on your plan's formulary.

- Ask for an exception if you or your prescriber believes that a coverage rule (like prior authorization) should be waived.

- Ask for an exception if you think you should pay less for a higher tier (more expensive) drug because you or your prescriber believes you can't take any of the lower tier (less expensive) drugs for the same condition.

> Definitions of blue words are on pages 125–128.

How do I ask for a coverage determination or exception?

You or your prescriber must contact your plan to ask for a coverage determination or an exception. If your network pharmacy can't fill a prescription, the pharmacist will give you a notice that explains how to contact your Medicare drug plan so you can make your request. If the pharmacist doesn't give you this notice, ask for a copy.

You or your prescriber may make a standard request by phone or in writing, if you're asking for prescription drug benefits you haven't gotten yet. If you're asking to get paid back for prescription drugs you already bought, your plan can require you or your prescriber to make the standard request in writing.

You or your prescriber can call or write your plan for an expedited (fast) request. Your request will be expedited if you haven't gotten the prescription and your plan determines, or your prescriber tells your plan, that your life or health may be at risk by waiting.

Important! ▶ If you're requesting an exception, your prescriber must provide a statement explaining the medical reason why the exception should be approved.

What are my rights if I think my services are ending too soon?

If you're getting Medicare services from a hospital, skilled nursing facility, home health agency, comprehensive outpatient rehabilitation facility, or hospice, and you think your Medicare-covered services are ending too soon, you can ask for a fast appeal. Your provider will give you a notice before your services end that will tell you how to ask for a fast appeal. The notice might call it an "expedited determination." You should read this notice carefully. If you don't get this notice, ask your provider for it. With a fast appeal, an independent reviewer, called a Beneficiary and Family Centered Care Quality Improvement Organization (BFCC-QIO), will decide if your services should continue.

How can I get help filing an appeal?

For more information about the different levels of appeals, visit Medicare.gov/appeals. You can also get help filing an appeal from your State Health Insurance Assistance Program (SHIP). See page 121 for the phone number.

What's an "Advance Beneficiary Notice of Noncoverage" (ABN)?

If you have Original Medicare, your doctor, other health care provider, or supplier may give you a notice called an "Advance Beneficiary Notice of Noncoverage" (ABN). This notice says Medicare probably (or certainly) won't pay for some services in certain situations.

What happens if I get an ABN?

- You'll be asked to choose whether to get the items or services listed on the ABN.
- If you choose to get the items or services listed on the ABN, you're agreeing to pay if Medicare doesn't.
- You'll be asked to sign the ABN to say that you've read and understood it.
- Doctors, other health care providers, and suppliers don't have to (but still may) give you an ABN for services that Medicare never covers. See page 61.

- An ABN isn't an official denial of coverage by Medicare. If Medicare denies payment, you can still file an appeal. However, you'll have to pay for the items or services if Medicare determines that the items or services aren't covered (and no other insurer is responsible for payment).

Can I get an ABN for other reasons?

- You may get a "Skilled Nursing Facility ABN" when the facility believes Medicare will no longer cover your stay or other items and services.
- You may get an ABN if you're getting equipment or supplies that are in the DMEPOS Competitive Bidding Program and the supplier isn't a contract supplier.

What if I didn't get an ABN?

If your provider was required to give you an ABN but didn't, in most cases, your provider must pay you back what you paid for the item or service.

Where can I get more information about appeals and ABNs?

- Visit Medicare.gov/appeals.
- Visit Medicare.gov/publications to view the booklet "Medicare Appeals."
- If you're in a Medicare plan, call your plan to find out if a service or item will be covered.

Your right to access your personal health information

By law, you or your legal representative generally has the right to view and/or get copies of your personal health information from health care providers who treat you, or by health plans that pay for your care, including Medicare. In most cases, you also have the right to have a provider or plan send copies of your information to a third party that you choose, like other providers who treat you, a family member, a researcher, or a mobile application (or "app") you use to manage your personal health information.

Definitions of blue words are on pages 125–128.

This includes:

- Claims and billing records
- Information related to your enrollment in health plans, including Medicare
- Medical and case management records (except psychotherapy notes)
- Any other records that contain information that doctors or health plans use to make decisions about you

You may have to fill out a health information "request" form, and pay a reasonable, cost-based fee for copies. Your providers or plans should tell you about the fee when you make the request. If they don't, you should ask. The fee can only be for the labor to make the copies, copying supplies, and postage (if needed). In most cases, you shouldn't be charged for viewing, searching, downloading, or sending your information through an electronic portal.

Generally, you can get your information on paper or electronically. If your providers or plans store your information electronically, they generally must give you electronic copies, if that's your preference.

You have the right to get your information in a timely manner, but it may take up to 30 days to fill the request.

For more information, visit hhs.gov/hipaa/for-individuals/guidance-materials-for-consumers/index.html.

How does Medicare use my personal information?

Medicare protects the privacy of your health information. The next 2 pages describe how your information may be used and given out, and explain how you can get this information.

Notice of Privacy Practices for Original Medicare

This notice describes how medical information about you may be used and disclosed and how you can get access to this information. Please review it carefully.

By law, Medicare is required to protect the privacy of your personal medical information. Medicare is also required to give you this notice to tell you how Medicare may use and give out ("disclose") your personal medical information held by Medicare.

Medicare must use and give out your personal medical information to provide information:

- To you, someone you name ("designate"), or someone who has the legal right to act for you (your personal representative)
- To the Secretary of the Department of Health and Human Services, if necessary, to make sure your privacy is protected
- Where required by law

Medicare has the right to use and give out your personal medical information to pay for your health care and to operate the Medicare Program. Examples include:

- Companies that pay bills for Medicare use your personal medical information to pay or deny your claims, to collect your premiums, to share your payment information with your other insurer(s), or to prepare your "Medicare Summary Notice."
- Medicare may use your personal medical information to make sure you and other people with Medicare get quality health care, to provide customer service to you, to resolve any complaints you have, or to contact you about research studies.

Medicare may use or give out your personal medical information for these purposes under limited circumstances:

- Where allowed by federal law to state and other federal agencies that need Medicare data for their program operations (like to make sure Medicare is making proper payments or to coordinate benefits between programs)
- To your health care providers so they know what other treatments you've gotten and to coordinate your care (for example, for programs to ensure the delivery of quality health care)
- For public health activities (like reporting disease outbreaks)
- For government health care oversight activities (like fraud and abuse investigations)
- For judicial and administrative proceedings (like in response to a court order)
- For law enforcement purposes (like providing limited information to locate a missing person)
- For research studies, including surveys, that meet all privacy law requirements (like research related to the prevention of disease or disability)
- To avoid a serious and imminent threat to health or safety
- To contact you about new or changed coverage under Medicare

- To create a collection of information that can no longer be traced back to you

By law, Medicare must have your written permission (an "authorization") to use or give out your personal medical information for any purpose that isn't set out in this notice. Medicare will not sell or market your personal medical information without your written permission. You may take back ("revoke") your written permission anytime, except to the extent that Medicare has already acted based on your permission.

By law, you have the right to:
- See and get a copy of your personal medical information held by Medicare.
- Have your personal medical information amended if you believe that it is wrong or if information is missing, and Medicare agrees. If Medicare disagrees, you may have a statement of your disagreement added to your personal medical information.
- Get a listing of those getting your personal medical information from Medicare. The listing won't cover your personal medical information that was given to you or your personal representative, that was given out to pay for your health care or for Medicare operations, or that was given out for law enforcement purposes if it would likely get in the way of these purposes.
- Ask Medicare to communicate with you in a different manner or at a different place (for example, by sending materials to a P.O. Box instead of your home address).
- Ask Medicare to limit how your personal medical information is used and given out to pay your claims and run the Medicare Program. Please note that Medicare may not be able to agree to your request.
- Be told about any breach of your personal medical information.
- Get a separate paper copy of this notice.

Visit Medicare.gov for more information on:
- Exercising your rights set out in this notice.
- Filing a complaint, if you believe Original Medicare has violated these privacy rights. Filing a complaint won't affect your coverage under Medicare.

You can also call 1-800-MEDICARE (1-800-633-4227) to get this information. Ask to speak to a customer service representative about Medicare's privacy notice. TTY users should call 1-877-486-2048.

You may file a complaint with the Secretary of the Department of Health and Human Services. Call the Office for Civil Rights at 1-800-368-1019. TTY users should call 1-800-537-7697. You can also visit hhs.gov/ocr/privacy.

By law, Medicare is required to follow the terms in this privacy notice. Medicare has the right to change the way any or all of your personal medical information is used and given out. If Medicare makes any changes to the way your personal medical information is used and given out, you'll get a new notice by mail within 60 days of the change.

The Notice of Privacy Practices for Original Medicare is effective September 23, 2013.

How can I protect myself from identity theft?

Identity theft happens when someone uses your personal information without your consent to commit fraud or other crimes. Personal information includes things like your name and your Social Security, Medicare, credit card, or bank account numbers. Guard your cards and protect your Medicare and Social Security numbers. **Keep this information safe.**

 If you suspect identity theft, or feel like you gave your personal information to someone you shouldn't have, call your local police department and the Federal Trade Commission's ID Theft Hotline at 1-877-438-4338. TTY users should call 1-866-653-4261. Visit ftc.gov/idtheft to learn more about identity theft.

How can I protect myself and Medicare from fraud?

Medicare fraud and abuse can cost taxpayers billions of dollars each year.

One common form of Medicare fraud is when a provider bills Medicare for services you never got. When you get health care services, record the dates on a calendar and save the receipts and statements you get from providers to check for mistakes. If you think you see an error or are billed for services you didn't get, take these steps to find out what was billed:

- Check your "Medicare Summary Notice" (MSN) if you have Original Medicare to see if the service was billed to Medicare. If you're in a Medicare health plan, check the statements you get from your plan.
- If you know the health care provider or supplier, call and ask for an itemized statement. They should give this to you within 30 days.
- Visit MyMedicare.gov to view your Medicare claims if you have Original Medicare. Your claims are generally available online within 24 hours after processing. You can also download your claims information by using Medicare's Blue Button. See page 117. You can also call 1-800-MEDICARE (1-800-633-4227). TTY users should call 1-877-486-2048.

Definitions of blue words are on pages 125–128.

If you've contacted the provider and you suspect that Medicare is being charged for a service or supply that you didn't get, or you don't know the provider on the claim, call 1-800-MEDICARE (1-800-633-4227). TTY users should call 1-877-486-2048.

For more information on protecting yourself from Medicare fraud and tips for spotting and reporting fraud, visit stopmedicarefraud.gov, or contact your local Senior Medicare Patrol (SMP) Program. See page 114.

You can also visit oig.hhs.gov or call the fraud hotline of the Department of Health and Human Services Office of the Inspector General at 1-800-HHS-TIPS (1-800-447-8477). TTY users should call 1-800-377-4950.

Plans must follow rules

Medicare plans must follow certain rules when marketing their plans and getting your enrollment information. They can't ask you for credit card or banking information over the phone or via email, unless you're already a member of that plan. Medicare plans can't enroll you into a plan over the phone unless you call them and ask to enroll, or you've given them permission to contact you.

Important!

Call 1-800-MEDICARE to report any plans that:

- Ask for your personal information over the phone or email
- Call to enroll you in a plan
- Use false information to mislead you

You can also call the Medicare Drug Integrity Contractor (MEDIC) at 1-877-7SAFERX (1-877-772-3379). The MEDIC helps prevent inappropriate activity and fights fraud, waste, and abuse in Medicare Advantage (Part C) and Medicare Prescription Drug (Part D) Programs.

What's the Senior Medicare Patrol (SMP) Program?

The SMP Program educates and empowers people with Medicare to take an active role in detecting and preventing health care fraud and abuse. There's an SMP Program in every state, the District of Columbia, Guam, the U.S. Virgin Islands, and Puerto Rico. Contact your local SMP Program to get personalized counseling, find out about community events in your area, or volunteer. For more information or to find your local SMP Program, visit smpresource.org, or call 1-877-808-2468. You can also call 1-800-MEDICARE (1-800-633-4227). TTY users should call 1-877-486-2048.

Fighting fraud can pay

You may get a reward if you help us fight fraud and meet certain conditions. For more information, visit stopmedicarefraud.gov or Medicare.gov, or call 1-800-MEDICARE.

Investigating fraud takes time

Every tip counts. Medicare takes all reports of suspected fraud seriously. When you report fraud, you may not hear of an outcome right away. It takes time to investigate your report and build a case, but rest assured that your information is helping us protect Medicare.

What's the Medicare Beneficiary Ombudsman?

An "ombudsman" is a person who reviews complaints and helps resolve them.

The Ombudsman reviews the concerns raised by people with Medicare through 1-800-MEDICARE and through your State Health Insurance Assistance Program (SHIP).

Visit Medicare.gov for information on how the Medicare Beneficiary Ombudsman can help you.

Definitions of blue words are on pages 125–128.

Section 10 —

Get More Information

Where can I get personalized help?

1-800-MEDICARE (1-800-633-4227)

TTY users call 1-877-486-2048

Get information 24 hours a day, including weekends

- Speak clearly, have your Medicare card in front of you, and be ready to provide your Medicare number.
- To enter your Medicare number, speak the numbers and letter(s) clearly one at a time. Or, enter your Medicare number on the phone keypad. Use the star key to indicate any place there may be a letter. For example, if your Medicare number is 000-00-0000A, you would enter 0-0-0-0-0- 0-0-0-0-*. The voice system will then ask you for that letter.
- Use 1 or 2 words to briefly say what you're calling about.

Helpful tips:

- You can say "Agent" at any time to talk to a customer service representative.
- If you need help in a language other than English or Spanish, or need to request a Medicare publication in an alternate format, let the customer service representative know.

Do you need someone to be able to call 1-800-MEDICARE on your behalf?

Important!

You need to let Medicare know in writing. You can fill out a "Medicare Authorization to Disclose Personal Health Information" form so Medicare can give your personal health information to someone other  than you. You can do this by visiting Medicare.gov/medicareonlineforms or by calling 1-800-MEDICARE (1-800-633-4227) to get a copy of the form. TTY users should call 1-877-486-2048. You may want to do this now in case you become unable to do it later.

Did your household get more than one copy of "Medicare & You?"

If you want to get only one copy in the future, call 1-800-MEDICARE. If you want to stop getting paper copies in the mail, visit Medicare.gov/gopaperless.

What are State Health Insurance Assistance Programs (SHIPs)?

SHIPs are state programs that get money from the federal government to give local health insurance counseling to people with Medicare at no cost to you. SHIPs aren't connected to any insurance company or health plan. SHIP volunteers work hard to help you with these Medicare questions or concerns:

- Your Medicare rights
- Billing problems
- Complaints about your medical care or treatment
- Plan choices
- How Medicare works with other insurance
- Finding help paying for health care costs

Definitions of blue words are on pages 125–128.

See page 121 for the phone number of your local SHIP. If you would like to become a volunteer SHIP counselor, contact the SHIP in your state to learn more. To find a SHIP in another state, visit shiptacenter.org or call 1-800-MEDICARE.

Where can I find general Medicare information online?

Visit Medicare.gov

- Get detailed information about the Medicare health and prescription drug plans in your area, including what they cost and what services they provide.
- Find doctors or other health care providers and suppliers who participate in Medicare.
- See what Medicare covers, including preventive services.
- Get Medicare appeals information and forms.
- Get information about the quality of care provided by plans, nursing homes, hospitals, home health agencies, and dialysis facilities.
- Look up helpful websites and phone numbers.

Where can I find personalized Medicare information online?

Register at MyMedicare.gov

- Manage your personal information (like medical conditions, allergies, and implanted devices).
- Sign up to get your "Medicare Summary Notices" (eMSNs) and this handbook electronically. You won't get printed copies if you choose to get them electronically.
- Manage your personal drug list and pharmacy information.
- Search for, add to, and manage a list of your favorite providers and access quality information about them.
- Track Original Medicare claims and your Part B deductible status.

Get access to your personal health information using Medicare's Blue Button. This feature lets you download 12–36 months of claims information for Part A and Part B and 12 months of claims information for Part D. This information can help you make more informed decisions about your care and can give your health care providers a more complete view of your health history. Visit MyMedicare.gov to use the Blue Button today.

How do I compare the quality of plans and providers?

Medicare collects information about the quality and safety of medical care and services given by most Medicare plans and health care providers. Medicare also has information about the experiences of people with the care and services they get.

Compare the quality of care and services given by health and prescription drug plans or health care providers nationwide by visiting Medicare.gov or by calling your State Health Insurance Assistance Program (SHIP). See page 121 for the phone number.

You can use the tools on Medicare.gov to get a "snapshot" of the quality of care and services some plans and providers give. Some of these tools feature a star rating system to help you compare plans and quality of care measures that are important to you. Find out more about the quality of care and services by:

- Asking what your plan or provider does to ensure and improve the quality of care and services. Each plan and health care provider should have someone you can talk to about quality.

- Asking your doctor or other health care provider what he or she thinks about the quality of care or services the plan or other providers give. You can also talk to your doctor or other health care provider about Medicare's information on quality of care and services.

Open Payments Program

Sometimes doctors and hospitals have financial relationships with drug, device, biological, and medical supply manufacturers. These relationships can include money for research activities, gifts, speaking fees, meals, or travel. Open Payments is a federally run transparency program that collects information about these financial relationships and makes it available to you so you can be more informed about how these relationships may impact your health care decisions. Visit CMS.gov/openpayments for more information.

Definitions of blue words are on pages 125–128.

What's Medicare doing to better coordinate my care?

Medicare continues to look for ways to better coordinate your care and to make sure that you get the best health care possible.

Here are examples of how your **health care providers** can better coordinate your care:

Electronic Health Records (EHRs)—EHRs are records that your doctor, other health care provider, medical office staff, or hospital keeps on a computer about your health care or treatments.

- EHRs can help lower the chances of medical errors, eliminate duplicate tests, and may improve your overall quality of care.
- Your doctor's EHR may be able to link to a hospital, lab, pharmacy, or other doctors, so the people who care for you can have a more complete picture of your health.

Electronic prescribing—This is an electronic way for your prescribers (your doctor or other health care provider who's legally allowed to write prescriptions) to send your prescriptions directly to your pharmacy. Electronic prescribing can save you money, time, and help keep you safe.

Accountable Care Organizations (ACOs)—An ACO is a group of doctors and other health care providers who agree to work together with Medicare to give you more coordinated service and care.

If you have Original Medicare and your doctor has decided to participate in an ACO, you'll know when you visit the office. A poster with information about your doctor's participation in an ACO will be displayed. At your request, the doctor will also give you this information in writing or you may get a letter in the mail.

The Health Insurance Portability and Accountability Act (HIPAA) Privacy Rule allows Medicare to share data with other entities as part of "health care operations." ACOs working with your doctors and other health care providers to coordinate service and care qualify as "health care operations." We have important safeguards to make sure the ACO uses the data appropriately.

The poster in your doctor's office will also let you know that Medicare will share certain information with the ACO about the care you got from your doctors and other providers. With the information Medicare shares, the doctors and health care providers in the ACO can have a complete picture of your health and be better able to coordinate your care.

You can ask Medicare not to share certain information with the ACO about the care you got from your doctors and other health care providers. To do this, call 1-800-MEDICARE (1-800-633-4227). TTY users should call 1-877-486-2048. and tell us you don't want us to share this information. You can change your data sharing preferences at any time.

Your Medicare benefits, services, costs, and protections won't change if your doctor participates in an ACO or if you prefer that Medicare not share your information. You still have the right to visit and get care from any doctor or hospital that accepts Medicare at any time, the same way you do now.

For more information, visit Medicare.gov/acos.html, or call 1-800-MEDICARE.

Are there other ways to get Medicare information?

Publications

Visit Medicare.gov/publications to view, print, or download copies of publications on different Medicare topics. You can also call 1-800-MEDICARE and say "Publications." Alternate formats are available at no cost. See page 13 for more information.

Social Media

Stay up-to-date and connect with other people with Medicare by following us on Facebook (facebook.com/Medicare.gov) and Twitter (twitter.com/MedicareGov).

Videos

Visit YouTube.com/cmshhsgov to see videos covering different health care topics on Medicare's YouTube channel.

Definitions of blue words are on pages 125–128.

Blogs

Visit blog.medicare.gov for up-to-date news from our website.

State Health Insurance Assistance Programs (SHIPs)

For help with questions about appeals, buying other insurance, choosing a health plan, buying a Medigap policy, and Medicare rights and protections.

This page has been intentionally left blank. The printed version contains phone number information. For the most recent phone number information, please visit shiptacenter.org, or call 1-800-MEDICARE (1-800-633-4227). TTY users should call 1-877-486-2048.

This page has been intentionally left blank. The printed version contains phone number information. For the most recent phone number information, please visit shiptacenter.org, or call 1-800-MEDICARE (1-800-633-4227). TTY users should call 1-877-486-2048.

This page has been intentionally left blank. The printed version contains phone number information. For the most recent phone number information, please visit shiptacenter.org, or call 1-800-MEDICARE (1-800-633-4227). TTY users should call 1-877-486-2048.

This page has been intentionally left blank. The printed version contains phone number information. For the most recent phone number information, please visit shiptacenter.org, or call 1-800-MEDICARE (1-800-633-4227). TTY users should call 1-877-486-2048.

Section 11 — Definitions

Assignment—An agreement by your doctor, provider, or supplier to be paid directly by Medicare, to accept the payment amount Medicare approves for the service, and not to bill you for any more than the Medicare deductible and coinsurance.

Benefit period—The way that Original Medicare measures your use of hospital and skilled nursing facility (SNF) services. A benefit period begins the day you're admitted as an inpatient in a hospital or SNF. The benefit period ends when you haven't received any inpatient hospital care (or skilled care in a SNF) for 60 days in a row. If you go into a hospital or a SNF after one benefit period has ended, a new benefit period begins. You must pay the inpatient hospital deductible for each benefit period. There's no limit to the number of benefit periods.

Coinsurance—An amount you may be required to pay as your share of the cost for services after you pay any deductibles. Coinsurance is usually a percentage (for example, 20%).

Copayment—An amount you may be required to pay as your share of the cost for a medical service or supply, like a doctor's visit, hospital outpatient visit, or prescription drug. A copayment is usually a set amount, rather than a percentage. For example, you might pay $10 or $20 for a doctor's visit or prescription drug.

Creditable prescription drug coverage—Prescription drug coverage (for example, from an employer or union) that's expected to pay, on average, at least as much as Medicare's standard prescription drug coverage. People who have this kind of coverage when they become eligible for Medicare can generally keep that coverage without paying a penalty, if they decide to enroll in Medicare prescription drug coverage later.

Critical access hospital—A small facility that provides outpatient services, as well as inpatient services on a limited basis, to people in rural areas.

Custodial care—Non-skilled personal care, like help with activities of daily living like bathing, dressing, eating, getting in or out of a bed or chair, moving around, and using the bathroom. It may also include the kind of health-related care that most people do themselves, like using eye drops. In most cases, Medicare doesn't pay for custodial care.

Deductible—The amount you must pay for health care or prescriptions before Original Medicare, your prescription drug plan, or your other insurance begins to pay.

Demonstrations—Special projects, sometimes called "pilot programs" or "research studies," that test improvements in Medicare coverage, payment, and quality of care. They usually operate only for a limited time, for a specific group of people, and in specific areas.

Extra Help—A Medicare program to help people with limited income and resources pay Medicare prescription drug program costs, like premiums, deductibles, and coinsurance.

Formulary—A list of prescription drugs covered by a prescription drug plan or another insurance plan offering prescription drug benefits. Also called a drug list.

Inpatient rehabilitation facility—A hospital, or part of a hospital, that provides an intensive rehabilitation program to inpatients.

Institution—For the purposes of this publication, an institution is a facility that provides short-term or long-term care, like a nursing home, skilled nursing facility (SNF), or rehabilitation hospital. Private residences, like an assisted living facility or group home, aren't considered institutions for this purpose.

Lifetime reserve days—In Original Medicare, these are additional days that Medicare will pay for when you're in a hospital for more than 90 days. You have a total of 60 reserve days that can be used during your lifetime. For each lifetime reserve day, Medicare pays all covered costs except for a daily coinsurance.

Long-term care—Services that include medical and non-medical care provided to people who are unable to perform basic activities of daily living, like dressing or bathing. Long-term supports and services can be provided at home, in the community, in assisted living, or in nursing homes. Individuals may need long-term supports and services at any age. Medicare and most health insurance plans don't pay for long-term care.

Long-term care hospital—Acute care hospitals that provide treatment for patients who stay, on average, more than 25 days. Most patients are transferred from an intensive or critical care unit. Services provided include comprehensive rehabilitation, respiratory therapy, head trauma treatment, and pain management.

Medically necessary—Health care services or supplies needed to diagnose or treat an illness, injury, condition, disease, or its symptoms and that meet accepted standards of medicine.

Medicare-approved amount—In Original Medicare, this is the amount a doctor or supplier that accepts assignment can be paid. It may be less than the actual amount a doctor or supplier charges. Medicare pays part of this amount and you're responsible for the difference.

Medicare health plan—Generally, a plan offered by a private company that contracts with Medicare to provide Part A and Part B benefits to people with Medicare who enroll in the plan. Medicare health plans include all Medicare Advantage Plans, Medicare Cost Plans, and Demonstration/Pilot Programs. Programs of All-inclusive Care for the Elderly (PACE) organizations are special types of Medicare health plans that can be offered by public or private entities and provide Part D and other benefits in addition to Part A and Part B benefits.

Medicare plan—Any way other than Original Medicare that you can get your Medicare health or prescription drug coverage. This term includes all Medicare health plans and Medicare Prescription Drug Plans.

Premium—The periodic payment to Medicare, an insurance company, or a health care plan for health or prescription drug coverage.

Preventive services—Health care to prevent illness or detect illness at an early stage, when treatment is likely to work best (for example, preventive services include Pap tests, flu shots, and screening mammograms).

Primary care doctor—The doctor you see first for most health problems. He or she makes sure you get the care you need to keep you healthy. He or she also may talk with other doctors and health care providers about your care and refer you to them. In many Medicare Advantage Plans, you must see your primary care doctor before you see any other health care provider.

Primary care practitioner—A doctor who has a primary specialty in family medicine, internal medicine, geriatric medicine, or pediatric medicine; or a nurse practitioner, clinical nurse specialist, or physician assistant.

Referral—A written order from your primary care doctor for you to see a specialist or get certain medical services. In many Health Maintenance Organizations (HMOs), you need to get a referral before you can get medical care from anyone except your primary care doctor. If you don't get a referral first, the plan may not pay for the services.

Service area—A geographic area where a health insurance plan accepts members if it limits membership based on where people live. For plans that limit which doctors and hospitals you may use, it's also generally the area where you can get routine (non-emergency) services. The plan may disenroll you if you move out of the plan's service area.

Skilled nursing facility (SNF) care—Skilled nursing care and rehabilitation services provided on a continuous, daily basis, in a skilled nursing facility. Examples of SNF care include physical therapy or intravenous injections that can only be given by a registered nurse or doctor.

TTY—A TTY (teletypewriter) is a communication device used by people who are deaf, hard-of-hearing, or have a severe speech impairment. People who don't have a TTY can communicate with a TTY user through a message relay center (MRC). An MRC has TTY operators available to send and interpret TTY messages.

Help in other languages

If you, or someone you're helping, has questions about Medicare, you have the right to get help and information in your language at no cost. To talk to an interpreter, call 1-800-MEDICARE (1-800-633-4227).

العربية (Arabic) إن كان لديك أو لدى شخص تُساعده أسئلة بخصوص Medicare فإن من حقك الحصول على المساعدة و المعلومات بلغتك من دون أي تكلفة. للتحدث مع مترجم إتصل بالرقم MEDICARE-800-1 (1-800-633-4227).

հայերեն (Armenian) Եթե Դուք կամ Ձեր կողմից օգնություն ստացող անձը հարցեր ունի Medicare-ի մասին, ապա Դուք իրավունք ունեք անվճար օգնություն և տեղեկություններ ստանալու Ձեր նախընտրած լեզվով: Թարգմանչի հետ խոսելու համար զանգահարեք 1-800-MEDICARE (1-800-633-4227) հեռախոսահամարով:

中文 (Chinese-Traditional) 如果您，或是您正在協助的個人，有關於聯邦醫療保險的問題，您有權免費以您的母語，獲得幫助和訊息。與翻譯員交談，請致電 1-800-MEDICARE (1-800-633-4227).

فارسی (Farsi) اگر شما، یا شخصی که به او کمک میرسانید سوالی در مورد اعلامیه مختصر مدیکردارید، حق این را دارید که کمک و اطلاعات به زبان خود به طور رایگان دریافت نمایید. برای مکالمه با مترجم با این شماره زیر تماس بگیریدMEDICARE-800-1 (1-800-633-4227).

Français (French) Si vous, ou quelqu'un que vous êtes en train d'aider, a des questions au sujet de l'assurance-maladie Medicare, vous avez le droit d'obtenir de l'aide et de l'information dans votre langue à aucun coût. Pour parler à un interprète, composez le 1-800-MEDICARE (1-800-633-4227)

Deutsch (German) Falls Sie oder jemand, dem Sie helfen, Fragen zu Medicare haben, haben Sie das Recht, kostenlose Hilfe und Informationen in Ihrer Sprache zu erhalten. Um mit einem Dolmetscher zu sprechen, rufen Sie bitte die Nummer 1-800-MEDICARE (1-800-633-4227) an.

Kreyòl (Haitian Creole) Si oumenm oswa yon moun w ap ede, gen kesyon konsènan Medicare, se dwa w pou jwenn èd ak enfòmasyon nan lang ou pale a, san pou pa peye pou sa. Pou w pale avèk yon entèprèt, rele nan 1-800-MEDICARE (1-800-633-4227).

Italiano (Italian) Se voi, o una persona che state aiutando, vogliate chiarimenti a riguardo del Medicare, avete il diritto di ottenere assistenza e informazioni nella vostra lingua a titolo gratuito. Per parlare con un interprete, chiamate il numero 1-800-MEDICARE (1-800-633-4227).

日本語 (Japanese) Medicare (メディケア) に関するご質問がある場合は、ご希望の言語で情報を取得し、サポートを受ける権利があります (無料)。通訳をご希望の方は、1-800-MEDICARE (1-800-633-4227) までお電話ください。

한국어(Korean) 만약 귀하나 귀하가 돕는 어느 분이 메디케어에 관해서 질문을 가지고 있다면 비용 부담이 없이 필요한 도움과 정보를 귀하의 언어로 얻을 수 있는 권리가 귀하에게 있습니다. 통역사와 말씀을 나누시려면 1-800-MEDICARE(1-800-633-4227)로 전화하십시오.

Polski (Polish) Jeżeli Państwo lub ktoś komu Państwo pomagają macie pytania dotyczące Medicare, mają Państwo prawo do uzyskania bezpłatnej pomocy i informacji w swoim języku. Aby rozmawiać z tłumaczem, prosimy dzwonić pod numer telefonu 1-800-MEDICARE (1-800-633-4227).

Português (Portuguese) Se você (ou alguém que você esteja ajudando) tiver dúvidas sobre a Medicare, você tem o direito de obter ajuda e informações em seu idioma, gratuitamente. Para falar com um intérprete, ligue para 1-800-MEDICARE (1-800-633-4227).

Русский (Russian) Если у вас или лица, которому вы помогаете, возникли вопросы по поводу программы Медикэр (Medicare), вы имеете право на бесплатную помощь и информацию на вашем языке. Чтобы воспользоваться услугами переводчика, позвоните по телефону 1-800-MEDICARE (1-800-633-4227).

Tagalog (Tagalog) Kung ikaw, o ang isang tinutulungan mo, ay may mga katanungan tungkol sa Medicare, ikaw ay may karapatan na makakuha ng tulong at impormasyon sa iyong lenguwahe ng walang gastos. Upang makipag-usap sa isang tagasalin ng wika, tumawag sa 1-800-MEDICARE (1-800-633-4227).

Tiếng Việt (Vietnamese) Nếu quý vị, hay người mà quý vị đang giúp đỡ, có câu hỏi về Medicare, quý vị sẽ có quyền được giúp và có thêm thông tin bằng ngôn ngữ của mình miễn phí. Để nói chuyện qua thông dịch viên, gọi số 1-800-MEDICARE (1-800-633-4227).

Please keep this handbook for future reference.

The information in "Medicare & You" describes the Medicare program at the time it was printed. Changes may occur after printing. Visit Medicare.gov or call 1-800-MEDICARE to get the most current information.

"Medicare & You" isn't a legal document. Official Medicare Program legal guidance is contained in the relevant statutes, regulations, and rulings.

U.S. DEPARTMENT OF
HEALTH AND HUMAN SERVICES

Centers for Medicare & Medicaid Services
7500 Security Blvd.
Baltimore, MD 21244-1850

Official Business
Penalty for Private Use, $300

CMS Product No. 10050
September 2016

National Medicare Handbook

Moving? Visit socialsecurity.gov, or call Social Security at
1-800-772-1213. TTY users should call 1-800-325-0778.
If you get RRB benefits, contact the RRB at 1-877-772-5772.
TTY users should call 1-312-751-4701.

¿Necesita usted una copia de este manual en Español?
Llame al 1-800-MEDICARE (1-800-633-4227).
Los usuarios de TTY deberán llamar al 1-877-486-2048.

Medicare cares about what you think. If you have
general comments about this handbook, email us at
medicareandyou@cms.hhs.gov. We can't respond to every
comment, but we'll consider your feedback when writing
future handbooks.

Made in the USA
San Bernardino, CA
10 May 2017